Top 50 Rules of Investing

"Scott Reed is a fiduciary advisor and a gifted writer. His book, *Top 50 Rules of Investing*, combines the ethos of comprehensive financial planning with the skills of individualized investment advice. Mr. Reed's subject includes the entirety of a life well-lived, and he accomplishes his goal in clear language, apt analogies, and in a loving and gentle manner."

"In over forty years in the investment world, I rarely see a book that has wisdom surpassing *Aesop's Fables*, and yet here Scott Reed provides positive suggestions and sound advice on how an investor can be future-focused and solution-oriented, and told with real-world stories that have timeless application."

"Scott Reed has done what I had always hoped to do, which is to condense invaluable wisdom within fifty highly readable, immensely helpful, rules. Kudos."

—Keith "Sunny" Loveland, 2010 Recipient, FPA Heart of Financial Planning Award

"Scott in *Top 50 Rules of Investing* has provided bite-size nuggets of money and investment advice. But he's also given us much more to sink our teeth into . . . Lessons on life and friendship, stories to learn from, and tidbits of wisdom wrapped inside amusing stories. With these 50 Rules, he's found the perfect way to share his knowledge. And I'm anxiously awaiting the next 50."

—Tom Brown, Radio and TV Host

"Scott often says: "Investing ain't rocket-surgery!" Ignore those fancy, but incomprehensible, investment schemes and advertisements for toogoodtobetrue financial products. Instead, ENJOY reading Scott's down-home yet PRACTICAL guide to those things that really make a difference, both in financial wellness and life in general."

—Barry Flagg, President, Founder and Inventor of Veralytic Inc.

"Scott Reed's 50 Rules provide meaningful and straightforward investment and life advice that applies notably to young professionals early in their career. Scott's guidance is invaluable to those just beginning their investment journey and can help propel both you (and your mental mind), as well as your portfolio, toward success."

—**Cannon Funderburk**, Practicing Attorney and Former Federal Law Clerk

TOP

50

RULES OF
INVESTING

AN ENGAGING AND THOUGHTFUL GUIDE DOWN
THE PATH OF SUCCESSFUL INVESTING PRACTICES

SCOTT REED

NEW YORK

LONDON • NASHVILLE • MELBOURNE • VANCOUVER

TOP 5 RULES OF INVESTING

An Engaging and Thoughtful Guide Down the Path of Successful Investing Practices

Published in New York, New York, by Morgan James Publishing. Morgan James is a trademark of Morgan James, LLC. www.MorganJamesPublishing.com

Proudly distributed by Publishers Group West®

Morgan James BOGO™

A **FREE** ebook edition is available for you or a friend with the purchase of this print book.

CLEARLY SIGN YOUR NAME ABOVE

Instructions to claim your free ebook edition:
1. Visit MorganJamesBOGO.com
2. Sign your name CLEARLY in the space above
3. Complete the form and submit a photo of this entire page
4. You or your friend can download the ebook to your preferred device

ISBN 9781636983752 paperback
ISBN 9781636983769 ebook
Library of Congress Control Number:
2023949780

Cover Design by:
Paul Mitchell
www.saintemblem.com

Interior Design by:
Chris Treccani
www.3dogcreative.net

Morgan James is a proud partner of Habitat for Humanity Peninsula and Greater Williamsburg. Partners in building since 2006.

Get involved today! Visit: www.morgan-james-publishing.com/giving-back

DEDICATION

To Dr. John Lachs, Professor of Philosophy at Vanderbilt University. Dr. Lachs seeded in me a desire to understand the importance of philosophy in my life and a desire to develop my own personal philosophy. I am eternally grateful to him for his wisdom and his ability to inspire a young student who was not easily inspired. Without John Lachs there might not be a *Top 50 Rules of Investing* and I would certainly be a much different and less inspired amateur philosopher of investing.

TABLE OF CONTENTS

FOREWORD

In my foreword to my original book, *Top 40 Rules of Investing*, I wrote, "There are certainly more than 40 Rules and if enough of you decide to read these and give them a shot, I will promise to write another book with more rules." Well, here we are! This second edition has become the *Top 50 Rules of Investing* with ten new rules.

I have listened to my readers who have said that they use my book much as a reference book, going back to read chapters when they apply to current situations. To make that process more productive we have added note pages to each chapter so you can make personal notes to refer to as well. We will also have a QR Code that will take you to our book website where you can find more information on the rules and videos where I discuss each rule in more detail.

The first edition was written to fill what I believe to be a huge void in investment literature and education, the philosophy behind good investment decisions. Most investment books want to tell you what to do or how to do it. How to implement a certain strategy that will make you rich or how to pick a stock that is going to soar. The goal of this book is to teach investors how to think. If you know how to think about investing, you can make better decisions no matter what your personal situation might be.

I think we all have shorter attention spans than we had when I started in the investment business so I have kept each chapter between 500 and 700 words so the reader can stay focused and pick the book up whenever they have a moment. Honestly it would make a great beach read. Not to take anything away from John Grisham but it is light weight, fits in as beach bag, and can be started and stopped at a moment's notice.

As I stated in my forward to the first edition, some of these rules were learned the hard way and some are based on empirical evidence and hard data. All of these rules have been confirmed be me in my almost 40-year journey as an investment advisor.

I hope you enjoy round two of my Rules of Investing!

RULE #1

Friends Are Worth More Than Money

"When the snows fall and the white winds blow,
the lone wolf dies but the pack survives."
—**George R.R. Martin,** *A Game of Thrones*

I t's almost eight o'clock on Wednesday night, the last night of April 2014. I am sitting at my desk at home using a light hooked up to my generator, staring at my iPad, and wondering what to say about investments. I can look out my window and see how much my life has changed. It only took a few seconds. I was here with my family huddled in a basement bathroom when it happened. An F3 tornado swept through our family property and took into the wind much of what I considered to be mine.

We were lucky. We were safe. Nevertheless, the shock of what Mother Nature had done to our family land was overwhelming. Ninety percent of the trees on our combined twelve acres of land were gone. The three family homes on our property were all significantly damaged. In only a matter of eighteen seconds the world I had known since birth was no longer the same.

After the tornado had passed, it only took a few minutes for my nephew to show up. He had run to us from his home nearby. Minutes later, one of my oldest friends showed up, crawling over tree trunks. Just an hour had gone by when my brother-in-law appeared, mud-streaked and soaking wet. His neighborhood was also hit, but they were spared and here he was.

During the balance of the afternoon, my children's youth minister, old friends from close by, and some from as far away as Oxford, made it to my house for no other reason than to help. Even more humbling were the people there whom I had never met. A man from Pontotoc showed up the next morning with a tractor and worked tirelessly from seven o'clock in the morning until seven o'clock at night. A crew of ten people with chainsaws and a forklift got to places that would have taken me days. My wife and children worked on the house with much help from old friends and very new friends. My daughters' friends showed up to help. At one time, I counted twenty chainsaws working within my eyesight. We cut a path to the main roads and cleared the driveways in front of the houses. It may sound cliché, but with all the devastation around me, all I could think about was how blessed I was and how rich I had become in my life. I know that there are good people and bad people in the world, but during a crisis it seems like the good people simply take over.

I am writing a book of rules for investors. I have been giving a lot of thought to which rule will be number one. Always invest with someone you trust is an easy one. Understand the risks involved is another. One will surely be to make sure that your advisor has your best interest as their primary goal. That is certainly what happened to me and my family this week.

People put our best interest above their own and made us their priority. But as I was thinking of things this evening, looking at a landscape that is forever changed and still looks more like a war zone than a backyard, I realized that there is only one right answer to the question of which rule will be first. The first rule of investing is to invest in your friends. I know that it may sound corny, and it doesn't have the pizazz of other investment ideas, but it is absolutely number one.

The hard and true fact of the matter is that if you have friends, the kind that will come to you when you need them, then you will never be poor. And if you aren't willing to share your life with others and become the kind of friend that will be there for your friends when they need you, then you will never be rich. Until you get that right, how much you put back for your retirement doesn't seem so important.

_____
_____
_____
_____
_____
_____
_____
_____
_____
_____
_____
_____
_____
_____
_____
_____
_____
_____
_____
_____
_____
_____
_____
_____
_____
_____
_____
_____
_____
_____

RULE #2

Invest In Others

"Life becomes harder for us, when we live for others,
but it also becomes richer and happier."
—Albert Schweitzer

C ommit a meaningful amount of time to making the place
you live better. Get involved through the local Chamber of
Commerce or through the United Way. Volunteer for the
Boy Scouts, Big Brothers/Big Sisters, the Boys and Girls Club, the
symphony, or the theater. It doesn't really matter how you decide
to get involved, just do it.

You will find that helping other people has a lot of hidden
benefits. Most people will tell you how good it makes them feel
to help others, but the big secret is how much it actually helps
you. You could be clearing debris from city streets (it's not just for
prisoners). You could be feeding people at the Salvation Army, or
you could be sitting on an investment committee deciding how

to invest people' donations in an appropriate way. Whatever your job, there is much to learn about living right, saving money, the cost of being wasteful, and the duty you have to those who are counting on you. The next thing you know, you are learning how to create realistic goals and assess risk from a different point of view that will flow over into your own investments.

When people are investing their own money they have a hard time being rational. People can talk themselves into just about anything and ignore the risk in lieu of the big payoff. Most people wouldn't imagine doing that with the money at the United Way. Recklessly losing money that was there to help people in need is simply unacceptable.

Volunteering forces people to use their rational, cognitive mind to solve problems. It allows them to see the success that comes from managing in the role of a fiduciary, the critical benefit for investors. It is no secret that institutional investments perform better than the investments of individuals. The Dalbar group puts out a study often that shows the gap between the returns of institutions and individuals. The last study I saw showed a difference of about 7 percent. That means that if you made 3 percent, the average institutional account would have made about 10 percent.

I believe the main reason for that difference is that people investing institutional money are forced to be objective and think about what is best for the institution. Learning how to make decisions with someone else's money will force you to be a better investor with your own money.

The great benefit to this rule is that you really can't help others without helping yourself as well. You can be community minded and selfish at the same time. It's a win for everyone.

_____
_____
_____
_____
_____
_____
_____
_____
_____
_____
_____
_____
_____
_____
_____
_____
_____
_____
_____
_____
_____
_____
_____
_____
_____
_____
_____
_____
_____
_____

RULE #3

Know Who You Are Working With

"To be yourself in a world that is constantly trying to make you something else is the greatest accomplishment."

—Ralph Waldo Emerson

R ule three sounds pretty easy. Know who you are working with. It's actually not that easy. Most of you have heard someone say, "Work with someone you trust." That is great advice and could almost be a rule all on its own. But that just isn't enough. The hard part in our business is finding someone you can trust that does what you need.

In the early 1990s, banks, brokerage firms, insurance companies, and pretty much anyone who could claim to be in the investment business were given free rein to title their business card any way they liked. When I got my Series 7 license in 1985, my first business card read "Stockbroker" and I was proud to be one. It doesn't say that now because I don't broker anything. I give advice for a fee and that is a much different relationship. The problem is that it has become more attractive to the client to be an advisor than a stock broker. So now you see a lot of business cards that say advisor or consultant and they may actually be doing neither.

You may say that your investment professional certainly gives you advice, and I am sure that is true, but what matters is what you have hired him/her to do. If you are like many investors, you don't need an advisor. You may want to make your own decisions and you need quality information on a timely basis from someone who can access any product that you may need. For that situation, you need a stockbroker. You may need information on various insurance products that would fit your lifestyle. An insurance broker would certainly fit the bill. These investment professionals do not, by definition, get paid to give you advice. They get paid to sell you investment products. You are the one responsible for making sure it is what you need.

To make things even more confusing, consultants and advisors are similar in our business, but traditionally there is one major difference. Consultants are paid to give you advice, but they do not normally take responsibility for their advice. The client is still the one who makes the final decision. Consultants give you their thoughts and let you decide if you are going to do what they think. Consultants shouldn't be selling products, even though often they do. When a consultant's best thought is also a product that was created by the consultant's company, you have to wonder if there is a conflict of interest that is getting in the way.

Advisors are paid to advise their clients on their investment portfolio and they do take on fiduciary responsibility for their advice. They are also required to keep up with those investments and provide ongoing advice. Only those professionals that take on fiduciary responsibility for their advice are required to keep up with their recommendations. Many advisors take on discretion for their clients and make the day-to-day decisions on their clients' behalf since they have a legal obligation to work in the client's best interest. They are expected to know what is in the client's best interest better than the client. That is a much different relationship.

So, if you want to make your own decisions and just need information, an advisor is not what you need. It may be hard to find what you need because so many people use *advisor* on their business card. If you need a more holistic approach, an advisor may be just right. At the end of the day, it is very hard to sell product and give advice. They are two different animals. The reverse is true as well. Finding someone you trust is critical to your ability to stay the course with your plan. But surely you can find someone you trust who is actually doing what you need them to do. That is the Holy Grail for the investor.

RULE #4

Don't Just Do Something, Sit There

"Patience is bitter, but its fruit is sweet."
—Jean-Jacques Rousseau

O ur society is changing. We have so many gadgets that are made to save us time that we spend all our time on those gadgets. People wear their ability to multitask like a badge of honor. Everyone, it seems, wants to be a doer. We want to quantify our worth in 60-hour weeks and how many things we can check off of our list.

It's no surprise that when it comes to investments, investors want to constantly be fiddling with things. The tendency to change those things that aren't working and trade them in for something that is working is very strong. Sadly, our industry, to a large extent, applauds us for changing. The majority of the professionals in our industry work on some sort of commission. That means they don't get paid unless you do something with your investments. There is nothing in it for them if you stay put. So they are constantly looking for things for you to do. The financial media would lose its audience if they came on the air every day and said, "Well, we can't really see anything that you need to do today."

I remember years ago when *CNBC* would bring a stock analyst on the show on Mondays to tout a stock and bring him/her back on Friday to see how it fared. The stock market game in schools gives play money to classrooms and they have a few months to "play" the stock market. Playing the stock market may be fun, but you shouldn't "play" the market with money that you are really counting on

With an investor's desire to fix things that seem broken, and an industry that, in many cases, encourages change, it is easy to see how things can get out of whack pretty quickly. It feels good to sell your losers and it feels good to buy winners. But you just can't overlook the fact that the investment business is a "reversion to the mean" business. More often than people would imagine, today's losers become tomorrow's winners and today's winners become tomorrow's losers

Good investing is less about feeling good and more about being good. Ben Hogan, one of golf's great players, once said about how to hold a golf club, "If it feels right then you are probably doing something wrong." Investing isn't much different.

Constant change in your portfolio creates more fees that have to be overcome in order to earn a profit. When you combine that with a strong tendency to buy things after they have become popular and their price has risen, and sell things after they have had bad news and their price has declined, then you implement a very costly plan: systematically buying high and selling low, instead of the other way around.

There are a lot of ways to make money on your investments. In my experience, the most consistently successful way is to put together a strategy that you can believe in and stick with it for a very long time. The challenge is to have faith in what you are doing and with whom you are doing it because you won't know if you are successful for a while. But that's okay, because it's not how you are doing today that matters, it's how you are doing when you need the money.

RULE #5

Interest Is A Weapon

"An atom blaster is a good weapon, but it can point both ways."
—Salvor Hardin

nyone who owns a credit card knows about interest. It's what you pay in order to borrow money from a bank to buy things. Anyone who has ever bought a Certificate of Deposit knows what interest is as well. It's what someone pays you for the right to use your money to loan out to someone else who will, in turn, pay them even more interest. And so it goes.

Interest is what makes millionaires and paupers. It can be the most positive or the most negative aspect of your financial life, depending on how you use it. Weapons are not inherently bad or good. A gun can be used by someone to break into your house and a gun can be used to stop someone from breaking into your house. The gun never changes. It is how someone uses the gun that changes. The same is true for interest.

17

Let's say that you bought $500 worth of goods and services on your credit card because you wanted things but didn't have the money to pay for those things all at once. The credit card company charges you 10 percent interest. You can afford to pay $100 on your card this month. So you pay $50 in interest and $50 down on what you owe. Next month, you buy something else and do the same thing. Now you are paying 10 percent interest on $950. Ninety-five dollars goes to interest and only five dollars goes to what you owe. You can see that it doesn't take long for that kind of money management to get out of control.

On the other hand, interest, or in this case a return on your investment, can work for you. If you invested $10,000 and made a return on your investment of 7 percent, you would have $700 at the end of the year. But next year, that same investment return would net you $749 because you are making 7 percent on both the money you invested and the money that you made on the investment, or $10,700. On and on it goes.

It is the magic of compounding your return or your loss. On the dark side, the more you owe at a certain interest rate, the worse off you are. The side of light and hope is just the opposite. The more you make . . . the more you make.

Most of us know someone who has let the compounding effect of interest affect them in a negative way. Things get so bad that they can't pay their bills and they end up filing bankruptcy. It's not uncommon. If it were, you wouldn't see so many bankruptcy commercials on TV. Looking back, I'm sure it is easy to see what went wrong.

"I shouldn't have bought that flat screen TV."

"I really didn't need that nice of a car."

"We shouldn't have gone to Hawaii last year."

It all adds up, and so does the interest.

What if you could turn that around? What if you could turn that interest you pay into a return on your money?

What if you said, "Instead of taking that trip this year, we are going to take a less expensive trip and put $500 into a college savings plan for the kids."

Or, "We are going to keep the TV we have and put $500 into our retirement plan."

If you start doing that, then the return on that money starts to compound and work for you, not against you. It may not seem like much at first, but as time goes on, it can make a huge difference in your financial life. Start today and let the miracle of compound interest work for you, not against you.

RULE #6

Investing Is Hard

"It takes a lot of time to gain experience."
—John C. Hardy

There are hundreds of commercials out there telling people how easy it is to invest. They will lead you to believe that investing is cheap and it is easy to do. I don't think that could be farther from the truth.

First of all, it is hard to be good at anything. I remember when I learned to tie my own tie. My dad worked with me for hours one Sunday afternoon until finally I got something that looked somewhat like a good Windsor knot. It was a long time before I could tie that knot easily. It was even longer until it looked right most of the time. And years later, I could tie a good knot in my car without the help of a mirror and know that it would look good. That is just one knot! I didn't become an expert on all kinds of knots.

I wasn't known as a tie expert. I was just trying to look good in a suit and tie.

In a study done a few years ago, I read that to become an expert in any endeavor takes about 10,000 hours of work. The tennis pros playing at Wimbledon have certainly put in that much time. It would be crazy to think you could play tennis three days a week for a couple of hours and beat one of those guys, even though you might have become a decent tennis player over time.

Now think about this: How good do you need to be to make the decisions that are going to affect your financial well-being for the rest of your life? Can you afford college for your children? Can you afford to retire while you can still enjoy retirement? Will you leave a legacy for your family?

These are pretty important questions. It doesn't seem reasonable to me to believe that your best shot at making those things happen is with an Internet account, some trading software, and an hour a day set aside to figure out your next major move.

If you spent forty hours a week learning how to invest well, it would take you four years and nine and a half months to get your 10,000 hours. At two hours a day, seven days a week, it would be almost fifteen years before you would gain expert status.

A lot of investors think the hard part is finding good investment opportunities. I would say that is one of the easier things to do. The hard part is knowing when to sell, when to hold, and when to buy more. There are a lot of moving parts to successful investing. Most of them should come with a warning label that says, "If you are investing your own money, you are probably using the wrong part of your brain to make the following decisions." There is a lot of evidence that people who manage their own money are much more emotional, and emotional decisions come from a different part of your brain than rational decisions.

Let's put it all together. If you are an investor who has decided to go it on your own, you have a very good chance that your investment advisor is not an expert in the field. He/she is probably using a part of his/her brain that tends to make poor rational decisions. That just doesn't sound like a very good way to go about managing something as important as your financial future.

Investing is hard. You need an expert to help you get it right.

RULE #7

Never Confuse Genius With A Bull Market

"A man's pride can be his downfall, and he needs to learn when to turn to others for support and guidance."
—**Bear Grylls**

I began the investment business on August 19th, 1985. The Dow Jones Industrial Average was the most watched index in the world at the time. It still is. It was trading at 1325. Since then, it has reached a high of 36,799. That is a lot of growth. There have been market corrections of a 10 percent or more drop almost yearly on average since then. There has been a Bear market on average every four years since then. And still the Dow Jones Average continues to rise. Each individual investor's part in that rise is simply insignificant, yet investors spend a lot of time trying to beat the markets.

It was interesting to me to hear people talk about what was happening to them in the down-market. I don't recall one single conversation where someone said, "I just picked the wrong stocks. If I had done a better job this wouldn't have happened to me. I must just be stupid." Instead, I heard people say, "What is happening to me? The banks caused this problem! If the Federal Government would do their job, none of this would have happened!" It was anyone else's fault but my own.

In up markets, which is about 70 percent of the time, the rhetoric is much different. Instead of, "Look what the market did to me!" They are now saying, "Look at how much money I made last year! Look at what my investments are doing! Look at how smart I am!"

It is natural to want to take credit for the good things that happen to you and blame someone else for the bad things, but it is dangerous to start believing that it is true. My father told me early in my career that I would do well to remember that when a client lost money, it was my fault, but when he made money, it was his "fault." My dad was right. That is a pretty accurate portrayal of how things have gone over the nearly four decades that I have been in the investment business.

It's all rather harmless until you start believing your own press and start making investment decisions based on the fact that you are an investment genius. There are very few financial geniuses in the world. I can count the ones I consider geniuses on one hand and that spans the past one hundred years. There are a lot of geniuses that invest, but that's different than being an investment genius. Most people that are cloaked in the appearance of genius are simply lucky. At some point, that luck will run out.

I believe in Proverbs 16:18. "Pride goes before destruction." Every time in my career that I began to think I knew more than everyone else, I found out that I was wrong. I am now very comfortable in knowing that I don't have the silver bullet of the investment world. I rely on empirical evidence and historical data to determine how to best invest. However, I have not given up on using my gut feelings. I just save them for ordering dinner.

_____
_____
_____
_____
_____
_____
_____
_____
_____
_____
_____
_____
_____
_____
_____
_____
_____
_____
_____
_____
_____
_____
_____
_____
_____
_____
_____
_____
_____
_____

RULE #8

What You Invest Trumps How You Invest

---

*"If you don't plant the seed, it doesn't matter
how well you till the soil."*
—Scott Reed

In our industry, we spend a lot of time talking, writing, and arguing about the next great investment idea. It is our nature and it is something that clients have come to expect from an investment professional. I write from time to time about the secrets of our industry. Those things that can help you reach your goals. Those things that only we know. We want you to believe that we are the answer to your prayers. We can make the difference in how you live your life.

But when it comes right down to it, you make the difference in your financial life. You are the one who decides what is important now and what is important later in life. I can't tell you if a 60-inch flat screen TV to watch the Super Bowl is more important than saving for college. I'm not at Best Buy or Wal-Mart when you are staring at the wall of TVs, dreaming of actually seeing that little yellow ball in high definition when you are watching Wimbledon. But that is where the rubber meets the road. Those everyday decisions are the difference between having enough for college, retirement, or your daughter's wedding. Yes, people are now beginning to start wedding accounts for their children.

I can put together a plan for you that should make what you do better over time, but how much you earn on your investments is directly tied to how much you invest. If you make 10 percent on your portfolio over the period of a year, I would consider that a good year. If you invested $1,000, you will have earned $100. If you invested $10,000, you will have earned $1,000. And if you had invested $100,000, you would have earned $10,000. All three portfolios had the same return, but the dollars you can spend are much different.

The point is that I can do a great job for you and you still won't get where you want to go if you don't commit yourself to the same plan. Making money is not what this is all about. It is about reaching goals.

If your investments only average 2 percent a year and you have managed to have all the money you need for college, retirement, vacations, etc., then you will have had a successful investment life. If, on the other hand, you have managed to make 12 percent a year for your entire life and still fall short of all your goals, then you have failed. Success has much more to do with your commitment to your financial plan than my commitment.

Don't get me wrong. I'm not saying that you don't need to invest. Remember the parable of the talents? I am not suggesting that you put your money under a rock. A good investment plan can make a big difference in you reaching your goals, but this is a team sport. You may need me in order to reach your goals, but I can assure you that I need you more. Just like the Tom Cruise line in the movie *Jerry Maguire*, "Help me help you!"

RULE #9

Find Your Comfort Zone
And Stay There

"The path of least resistance has a lot going for it. The comfort zone isn't where you lose yourself. It's where you find yourself."

—Meghan Daum

Your tolerance to risk is a critical component of getting your investment plan right. Investors hear advisors talk a lot about the idea that the more risk you take, the more money you make. Many pundits in the financial press try to lure you in with tales of doubling your money in a few weeks and target prices that will triple the price of the stock. I won't lie to you and tell you that those investments don't exist, but I will tell you that it usually only works on paper. I can put a hundred hypotheticals in front of you that will show you how much money you can make if you will only take the risk.

33

For example, we know that over a long period of time, Emerging Market stocks beat small cap stocks and small cap stocks beat large cap stocks. The problem is that in order to get those returns, you have to leave the investments alone and let them do their thing. That strategy almost never happens. Investors just can't stop messing with their investments. They get greedy they get scared and they make decisions that are bad for their portfolio at an astonishing rate.

When you are in an investment that has big swings that take you away from your comfort zone, it just causes all kinds of problems. At the end of the day, if you are the boss of your own investments, you have to overcome the fact that the markets will beg you to do the wrong thing at the wrong time. When stocks fall, there is a great tendency to look at your portfolio and think about how much you have lost and how much more you don't want to lose instead of thinking about how cheap the underlying securities have become and how good it would be to buy some more at this cheap price.

Just as punishing is the fact that as an investment goes up, investors should be taking money off the table and lowering their risk. But who wants to sell an investment that is on its way up? Greed kicks in and those investments tend to be held until they turn around and start heading down. Then the tendency is to hold the investment until it gets back to its previous high. Often that doesn't happen. You may watch it go down and down and down. This scenario plays out over and over in the investment world. Every professional I know has stories about clients that have self-destructed in this way.

Being able to tolerate the risk of a portfolio without making decisions that will hurt you is the only way I know to get the results in those hypotheticals. Think hard about trying to get more return than you can stand because those returns aren't meant for you. They are meant for someone who can stand the risk. The only way I know to maximize your returns over time is to find your true comfort zone and stay there.

RULE #10

Creating Wealth Is Different From Maintaining Wealth

---

*"The first step toward change is awareness.
The second step is acceptance."*
—Nathaniel Branden

Most investors think that investing is all about making money. That thought isn't exactly true. Investing is about creating a better life, reaching goals, and attaining peace of mind. It is the attitude of most investors that I have worked with that making money is the way to reach goals, create a better life, and attain peace of mind, but I have found that not to be an innate truth.

There is so much more to the success of an investment plan than simply seeing how much money you can make. Understanding your investment cycle is crucial to your long-term success. You can divide your investment process into two main phases: The

Wealth Creation Phase and The Wealth Maintenance Phase. For a much higher chance of long-term success you have to realize when you switch from one to the other. For some, that shift can be very swift and for others, it can take a while. Most of us ease from one to the other as we get older.

We realize that we need to be protecting our assets as much as we need to be growing our assets. But the change can come quickly to those that have had an accident, injury, or other issue that forces them out of the working world. That is one reason that communication with your investment professional is so critical. They can help you realize major shifts that require a change in strategy.

The creation of wealth is a much different mindset than the maintenance of wealth. In The Creation Phase of your investment life, which most boomers like myself have put astern, there is a need to take risks and an ability to overcome those risks. Losing 30 percent of $10,000 at age twenty-five is not as devastating as losing 30 percent of $200,000 at age fifty-five. The percent of loss is the same in both scenarios, but the recovery time is what will get you if you are in The Maintenance Stage.

You can overcome the $3,000 loss in the first scenario by getting a part-time job for a while until you replace the money. Losing $60,000 at age fifty-five may cause you to rethink how and when you may retire. This becomes a problem for those investors that have been successful risking their investments over the early part of their investing career and have become desensitized to the risk. There is a strong tendency to continue doing what you have been doing, which can be a very dangerous game plan. It's hard to make changes in the way you are doing things, especially when you have been successful, but that is exactly what you should do. Taking risks will catch up with you.

Understanding that you will (not may) have a bad run is important. Changing your portfolio so that a bad run doesn't devastate your plan is just plain smart. I'm not saying that you should hide your money under a mattress once you can see the finish line. I am saying that taking an appropriate amount of risk is critical. If doubling your money won't change your lifestyle but losing 50 percent would, why would you take that risk? Pay attention to what phase your investment plan is in and act accordingly.

RULE #11

Fight The Current War,
Not The Last One

*"Losers live in the past. Winners learn from the past and enjoy
working in the present toward the future."*

—Denis Waitley

There is a crazy thing that goes on in the mind of almost every
investor that I know. It is called anchoring. Anchoring is when
an investor refuses to let go of something that has happened
and is willing to attach meaning to an event where there may be no
meaning. Then they take this often meaningless event and use it to
make future decisions. In other words, they drop their anchor and
refuse to make objective decisions that will move their financial
boat forward because they are hooked to this emotional anchor.

For example, a guy buys a stock at $25 per share with the hope
that it will go to $35 per share. The stock rises to $33. He doesn't

sell it because he is already set on $35. The stock drops back to $30. He doesn't want to sell it now because he knows that it has already reached $33, so it should at least get back there. He now anchors at $33.

The stock drops to $28. He now says, "I can't sell it in the twenties. It has been as high as $33. Just to save face I need to get $30." His new anchor is $30. The stock drops to $24. Now he says, "There is no way I'm selling this at a loss. I'm going to make a profit on this stock no matter how long it takes." Now his new anchor is $26.

Not once in that conversation did he really want to know the current condition of the stock. He hasn't asked why it is going down, or for that matter, why it went to $33 in the first place. It is all about the price.

You may think that this scenario sounds funny, but it plays out over and over again with investors everywhere. Human nature gets in the way of objective decision making and things that really don't matter at all become the most important factors in the decision-making process. Legacy stocks may be the most anchored stocks in the investment world.

Legacy stocks are stocks that you own for a reason other than your current investment plan. Legacy stocks could be stocks that were given to you by your parents or grandparents. It could be the first stock you ever owned. It may be stock in the company where you work. Legacy stocks are a problem for investors. Because they never want to sell them and because they tend to buy more of them, they can become too big a part of the portfolio. I have had conversations with clients where I suggested that they sell a good bit of their legacy stocks to get their portfolio back in line with their risk level and they refuse. I then ask them, "If you had cash to invest, would you buy this much of this stock?" They virtually always say, "Of course not!" Well, if you wouldn't buy it, why wouldn't you sell it?

The problem with anchoring is that it is a very natural thing to do. The problem with investing well is that you are required to do so many things that do not feel natural. Don't let anchoring get you down. Sorry, I couldn't resist the pun.

_____
_____
_____
_____
_____
_____
_____
_____
_____
_____
_____
_____
_____
_____
_____
_____
_____
_____
_____
_____
_____
_____
_____
_____
_____
_____
_____
_____
_____
_____

RULE #12

Fight The Noise

"More voices means less trust in any given voice."
—Eli Pariser

There is financial noise everywhere. Everyone knows about *CNBC* and *Bloomberg*. They know about the *Wall Street Journal*, *Fortune*, *Forbes*, *Money*, and a whole host of magazines that want to tell you what you should know. They all have smart people talking about important events. Often, I see really smart people who disagree with each other. Those disagreements make it hard to know who to believe. The most frustrating part of it all is that most of the financial news stories I read want me to believe that what they say actually matters to me. They don't even know me. How can they be so sure that I need to pay attention to them?

I remember years ago having an investor call me for advice. He wanted to get out of everything because he was convinced that the stock market was going down. I asked him to bring in a statement of what he owned so we could have a better conversation about his concerns. When reading his statement, I realized that he didn't own any stocks. All he was invested in were bonds. He had been listening to the news and it sounded so bad that he couldn't take it anymore even though he had no exposure to the thing everyone was worried about. That's like not eating corn because of the recent scare in the hog market. They are both commodities, but that's about where the similarities end.

Back in the eighties, there was still limited access to the investing world and the financial news seemed to provide more substance and less entertainment. Thanks to the access workers have to the financial markets through their retirement plans, almost everyone is in the financial markets. With that access comes interest and with that interest comes competition for your attention. With that competition comes a lot of financial entertainment pretending to be news. There is a lot of white noise out there that gets in the way of making good financial decisions.

Maria Sharapova is one of the great tennis players of all time. She has won the Career Grand Slam and has five major championships to her credit. Over the past ten years, she has consistently been ranked in the top ten tennis players and rated as high as number one. She has a ritual of facing away from the tennis court between points to give herself a moment to refocus on what is important. She said that it is too easy to get distracted from what you are supposed to be doing and to let other people control the tempo and direction of your game.

It is crucial to stay focused on what is important to you. You can't know everything. Just because everything matters doesn't mean everything matters to you. Determine where you need to focus your effort and energy and then fight all that noise out there that is trying to take you away from where you need to be.

RULE #13

Everyone Is A Business Owner

*"Planning is as natural to the process of success as
its absence is to the process of failure."*
—Robin Sieger

I t is the lifetime dream of so many Americans. We are hardwired
to believe in the American dream of owning our own business.
What a lot of people don't realize until it is too late is that we
all are business owners. We all own the business of taking care of
ourselves. It is one of the reasons why we save money.

We start out like most businesses, having very little money.
We have to borrow to get by and often flounder during those early
years when there is little responsibility and the mistakes are easier
to overcome. Once we start a family, it becomes more compli-
cated. Now money is going toward new clothes and more food.
The list goes on. We still have to save because we know that our
company isn't going to be big enough to support us if we don't

invest in it. We know that we will need raises along the way to take care of increased expenses. We also know that the more money we put in our company, the faster it will grow.

The ultimate goal of each of our companies is to be big enough to support its one employee and his/her family when we become full-time employees. If you haven't figured it out yet, I will become a full-time employee of Scott Reed Family, LLC when I retire. When I retire I will have to depend on the money I have saved and invested to pay my salary for the rest of my life. Many of the people I have talked with think of retirement money as money that you can spend, but that isn't how I think of it. I think of retirement money as the assets of my company, Scott Reed Family, LLC.

If I spend all of my assets, my company will fail. I have to spend a small portion every year on my salary so my company will continue to thrive for as long as I live. If I pay myself a small percentage of my assets, say 4 percent, then I can expect my company to continue to grow. If I buy a lake house and a Porsche with my assets, then all bets are off. If my company is strong when I am gone, then I can merge my company with my children's companies and that will make their company stronger.

You may think that it is silly to play word games with your investments, but I have found that people don't tend to make great decisions with their money when they think of it as their own. Greed and fear tend to get in the way of a good financial plan. If you can stop thinking about your savings and investments as your money and begin to think of it as its own business, you will have a better shot at making good decisions for your future self.

Statistics tell us that most new companies fail in the first five years. It's not easy to start a business. There will be mistakes and there will be triumphs. The key is to go ahead and get started building your business. The sooner you start, the better the chance that your business will be where it needs to be when you become its only full-time employee.

RULE #14

Get A Life

"Most people have no idea of the giant capacity we can immediately command when we focus all of our resources on mastering a single area of our lives."
—Tony Robbins

I see a lot of investors that spend a great deal of time managing their investments. They want to be involved in every aspect of the investment process from portfolio construction, to security research, to trading. That's a pretty hard thing to do, especially if you are counting on that money to enhance your retirement or your children's college education. You can't afford to be wrong.

Rule #6 mentions the fact that it takes about 10,000 hours to become an expert at any endeavor. The idea that people working a full time job would have enough time to put into the investment process to become an expert, and still have enough time left to have a life worth spending their investments on, is a hard sell to me. I don't know how you can do it all and do it all well. I think it is just fine to take some of your wealth and do what you want. Just don't do that with your "serious" money. The problem with investing is that it can be a fun game or it can be a serious process. Don't confuse the two.

In the early stages of my career, I spent a lot of time researching and picking stocks for my clients. When I moved to the consulting side of the business, I realized that I didn't have the time it took to be good at both consulting on the entire portfolio and picking the individual securities as well. Something had to go, so I quit picking securities. I think I could still be pretty good at it, but no matter how smart you might be, you probably won't be successful if you don't have the time to commit to the process.

I lost a great friend and a cousin recently. I could say it was expected, but anytime someone dies at the age of fifty-nine, it isn't expected. When I lose someone close to me, I tend to look back at their life and see what I have learned. Robert would frustrate me because I wanted him to be more driven. He was enormously smart and capable of anything, but it was not in his DNA to overachieve. One of our relatives said that Robert wanted to have fun and he wanted you to have fun as well. Relationships were very important to Robert. My daughters adored him. I think he liked my wife more than me. He had friends everywhere. We/I tend to talk a good game about how our relationships are the most important thing in our lives. Most of us don't walk the walk as hard as we talk the talk. We could use some practice. I realized that, since we were kids, Robert had helped me walk that walk much better than I ever would have on my own.

Studies show that a lot of individual investors tend to underperform over time. If you have to choose between work, which is pretty important to survival, relationships, which are pretty important to happiness, and managing your own investments, choose the first two. Hire out the investments and get a life!

RULE #15

Don't Chase The Hot Dot

"Realize what you really want. It stops you from chasing butterflies and puts you to work digging gold."
—William Moulton Marston

O ne of my daughters came into my study the other night to inform me that she had saved me 70 percent on a pair of shoes. She was very excited. I wanted to stop her and explain that because she didn't really need a pair of shoes, she didn't actually save me any money. She cost me that 30 percent that she actually paid. But that is a subject for another chapter. The point of the story is that my teenage daughters have become very astute at shopping for deals. They understand the value of buying quality merchandise at a reasonable price. And every now and then, they get to buy quality merchandise at a very cheap price. That is exciting.

The investment world tends to do just the opposite. The higher the price of a security, the more people want to buy it.

Many investors will gladly pay high prices for a stock for fear that they will be left behind. They see other investors making a lot of money on a stock and they want to do that as well. The problem is that by the time you find out about a hot stock, the gains have already been made by someone else.

We call that "chasing the hot dot." We want whatever is hot. But what we should want is whatever is about to go up, and that is a totally different thing. Finding diamonds in the rough is not easy. Chasing someone else's gains is easy. It is much more fun to talk about owning a piece of the hottest stock out there than trying to explain why you are really excited about buying stock in a company that no one cares about.

It is so easy to let emotions get in the way of a perfectly good investment plan. The Dalbar Group puts out a study each year that looks at individual investor performance versus institutional investor performance. Over the past twenty years or so that I have been following Dalbar, they show that individual performance is significantly less than their institutional counterparts. Most of that underperformance can be linked to the fact that individuals let their emotions invade their investment process and institutions usually don't. It is much easier to be reasonable when investing someone else's money than when investing your own (Rule #2).

In order to find great bargains in the investment world, you have to use the same mentality my teenage daughters use when shopping for deals. They know that the price is the highest when everyone is talking about something. They also know that if they keep their eye on something they want that, sooner or later, demand will wane and the price will drop. They determine what price they want to pay and when it gets there, they buy. If they really want something, then they want people to stop talking about it.

Increased demand equals increased price. They don't want to chase the hot dot. They want to chase the really cool dot that no one has noticed. Maybe you should do the same.

_____
_____
_____
_____
_____
_____
_____
_____
_____
_____
_____
_____
_____
_____
_____
_____
_____
_____
_____
_____
_____
_____
_____
_____
_____
_____
_____
_____

RULE #16

Start Now

"What must be done eventually should be done immediately."
—Jeremy Foley

I was having a conversation with two of my nephews the other night. They are both young, married, and thinking about having children. One is thinking about that more than the other. He already has two twin girls about a quarter of a year old. One of them asked me when I began saving money for my children. I told them that I had tried to open an account for my first daughter before she was even born and found that to be illegal. There have been huge disagreements over the years on when life actually begins, but I can tell you that the IRS is pretty clear that life doesn't begin until after birth if you are looking for a tax break.

There is an old saying in the investment world that goes, "Time in the markets is more important than timing the market." So many people I talk with tell me they want to wait until they have

61

more money before they begin to invest. That is the easy way out and there never seems to be a good time to start. Investing should be a bit painful. You have to give up immediate gratification for greater gratification down the road. It's all about compounding your return over time. I consider compounding your return as one of the great wonders of the world, right after the pyramids.

Let me put this in real terms. If my nephew starts an investment account for his girls right now, puts back $200 each per month, and is able to earn 8 percent a year in his investments, by the time his girls get out of college at age twenty-two, their accounts would be worth $139,000 each. If he waits until they are age twelve to start saving and puts the same amount of money back per month, those accounts would be worth only $36,000. That's a significant difference.

Let's talk about how this subject relates to retirement. Few people I have known are excited about putting money back in their retirement plan when they are in their twenties. It's hard to imagine retirement at that age and it is easy to imagine going to concerts, the beach, the mountains . . . anything other than retirement. It is important to understand what you are giving up by waiting to invest for retirement.

By putting back $2,000 per year for retirement beginning at thirty five years old, at 8 percent per year return, you would have a value in your retirement plan of $243,000 when you reach sixty five. If you were willing to start that program when you were twenty five, your market value would balloon to $556,000. Take that one step further: if you work for a company that matches your contribution 100 percent on that $2,000, you could be a millionaire by age sixty five.

You can feel a lot of things when it comes to investing. You can feel like it's not a good time. You can feel like you'll be able to catch up later. You can feel like things will be different, but math is math and numbers don't lie. The feeling I suggest that makes the most sense is the feeling that you need to start investing now.

RULE #17

It's A Top Down Process

"I paint from the top down. From the sky, then the mountains, then the hills, then the houses, then the cattle, and then the people."
—Grandma Moses

Most of the investors I talk to are very interested in finding that next great investment. They scour the Internet. They watch *CNBC*, *Bloomberg*, and *Kramer* in hopes of finding the next investment that they can add to their portfolio. Some people spend hours each day looking for that next investment opportunity.

What is interesting to me is that so many investors spend so little time on the things that I would consider to be more important to the investment process than picking the investments. Listed in importance to your long-term success, I would put individual investment selection somewhere around the top of the second page. It should be one of the last things you do to fulfill your investment plan.

On my list, the first thing to do is to decide if you want to go it alone or get some help. I have written about this quite a bit. There is no wrong answer to this question, but you have to be willing to commit the time and effort if you choose to go it alone. If you want help, you have to decide what kind of help you want. Do you want someone to feed you ideas and make commissions off of the products they sell you? Or do you want someone who is charged with helping you implement your plan? Someone who has a legal obligation to do what is in your best interest? That is a big decision and not as easy as you might think.

The second thing to do is put together your Investment Policy Statement. Everyone needs a road map. This is where you put in writing how you want to invest your money. It has nothing to do with any individual investment, but it is where you state the things you will do and those things you won't do. For instance, you may not want to invest in gold, so you exclude gold from your Investment Policy. Then when you see those commercials about how much money you can make on gold, you can change channels because you already know that you won't be doing that unless you change your Investment Policy Statement. It is a great way to stop yourself from making bad, emotional decisions.

The third thing to do is to create your investment model. You still have not given any thought to what investments you might buy. You are creating a model that incorporates all of the decisions you make in your Investment Policy Statement. You'll decide how much you should invest in stocks, how much in bonds, how much in other alternative investments, and more. At the end of this part of the process, you should know exactly what your ideal investment model looks like.

Finally, when you have finished putting together your investment model, you can look at funding your investment model with some investments. You look at each asset class and determine how best to fund that asset class. The great thing about this process is that it keeps you in line.

If your investment model says that you should only invest 8 percent in small cap growth stocks and you already have 8 percent, then you know that when *Kramer* is pitching a small cap growth stock, it doesn't apply to you. You can focus on the things that need focus instead of joining many of your investing brethren in their random walk through the investing world.

The last piece of the investment process is to develop a process for monitoring your investments. How are you going to grade your investments? How often are you going to grade your investments? Put a plan in place that will keep you on track. Then you do what they say on every shampoo bottle: rinse and repeat.

_____

_____

_____

_____

_____

_____

_____

_____

_____

_____

_____

_____

_____

_____

_____

_____

_____

_____

_____

_____

_____

_____

_____

_____

_____

_____

_____

_____

_____

_____

RULE #18

Cost Always Matters

"But nothing's really free, is it? People always make you pay one way or another."
—Jane Lotter, The Bette Davis Club

I really don't know why so many investors tend to ignore the costs of investing money. It could be that the excitement and lure of making a lot of money so far outweighs the tedious detail of determining if your costs are reasonable that many think it is just not worth it. I mean, who cares how much it is going to cost if the returns are big enough? It could also be that the financial services industry has been enormously effective at hiding investment costs inside the investment vehicles. It is sometimes very difficult to find the true cost of an investment. But at the end of the day, you can't get past the fact that costs matter and they matter a lot.

Costs matter so much that the Department of Labor has begun to require retirement plans to disclose their costs in a disclosure statement each year. This makes it much easier for the plan fiduciaries to determine how much they are paying. The Department of Labor realized that many plans were paying too much. The main reason for that was that they really didn't know what they were paying or how that compared to other plans.

If you don't believe me, all you have to do is look at the numbers. I took a portfolio worth $90,000 and gave it a 6 percent return over the next thirty years. I assumed a 1 percent cost and then begin to whittle away at the costs. If you were able to lower your cost from 1 percent to 0.75 percent, you would have an extra $30,000 at the end of thirty years. If you could lower the cost to 0.50 percent, you would have an extra $64,000. And if you could get it down to 0.25 percent, your account would grow an extra $90,000. That is a lot of money left on the table just because you didn't want to take the time to find out how much you were paying. It would be nice if someone were watching out for you, but that is not something you can count on.

The great majority of investment professionals in our industry will not take on a fiduciary role with their clients. Although there has been an effort in Congress to require non-fiduciaries to have greater responsibility, called best interest, it is still not a fiduciary standard. You should be wary of believing that it is adequate. At the end of the day, you have to take responsibility for either working under a fiduciary contract or taking the responsibility for understanding the products you are using and what they cost, all on your own.

I am not saying that high costs are always bad. There are times when paying up for an investment makes sense. If you are in a job that has a high risk of law suits, such as doctors, and an expensive investment like a variable annuity might be protected from litigation, then it might make sense.

If your portfolio needs to be diversified into some alternative spaces, such as hedge funds, then for that reason you may need to pay up. It is important to know when the time is right to pay up and make an educated decision to do so. It will make a huge difference in the long run and your portfolio will thank you.

RULE #19

Everything Changes

"Reversion to the mean is the iron rule of the financial markets."
—John Bogle

There is a mantra that I say over and over almost daily when it comes to investments. "It's a reversion to the mean business." That mantra never meant more to me than in the middle of 2008, when the equity markets were crashing all around us. I knew that eventually the markets reflect their true value and not the emotional value that is reflected in the day-to-day returns. It also allowed me to remember, in the years after the Great Recession, that the markets don't continue to go up without experiencing declines in the process.

Investors, in my experience, tend to extrapolate whatever is happening to them to a point that doesn't make sense. I remember an investor telling me toward the end of 2008 that he feared the Dow Jones Industrial Average could go to zero. Well, the Dow didn't even start at zero. There is always value, even if it is just in the desks and copy machines left in the businesses that we value.

On the other end of the spectrum is Bernie Ebbers. In the middle of Worldcom's great run, I asked him what his forecast for the next ten years would be for Worldcom's growth. He looked at me seriously and said he thought that Worldcom could continue along the same growth projection as it had been. That growth would have made Worldcom the largest company in the world in just about five years. It was an impossible feat.

Sometimes people just forget to do the math. Take a look at stocks over the long run. Stocks have averaged around a 10 percent annual return for a long time. Long-term numbers have meat to them because they are not emotionally based. They reflect more of the true economics of the markets. But if you look back at the last one hundred years, I don't think there has been one year where the stock market averaged exactly 10 percent. Some years are less, some are more. That means if the stock market is performing under 10 percent, you can expect to see it average more than 10 percent at some point.

The same is true when the stock market outperforms. It will have to come back to its long-term average eventually unless there has truly been a paradigm shift in how we value the markets, and that is a dangerous thought. Sir John Templeton would agree. He famously said, "The four most dangerous words in investing are, "This time is different."

Reversions happen all the time in the markets. Interestingly, I have observed that investors tend to believe that they deserve the upside shifts and don't deserve the downside. I think we would all do well to simply understand that a reversion to the mean is to be expected and not make big changes in the way we invest based on the markets doing what they are supposed to do.

A sailor sets sail for a new destination with his heading straight. He knows that there is no way that his boat will sail straight to its point. It will get blown off coarse often, but the captain simply reverts back to his original heading. He doesn't believe that the world map has changed simply because there is a strong wind from the North. He believes in his course. Successful investors tend to do the same thing.

RULE #20

Trust, But Verify

---

*"Doubt the conventional wisdom unless
you can verify it with reason and experiment."*
—Steve Albini

Trust, but verify. It's an old Russian proverb. However, it gained its place in the American lexicon for its use by President Ronald Reagan in 1986 to explain his position on Russian Nuclear Disarmament to then-President Mikhail Gorbachev. Reagan explained that it was not a lack of trust in the Russians, but a policy of his to always verify no matter how much he trusts his source.

What a great policy. He managed to take away all of the emotional issues attached to a lack of trust and put the emphasis on verifying what we already believed to be true.

There should be more of that in the investment world. Many investors believe that just because they trust the person they are seeing face to face that they need not do any more. That argument may hold water if the person you are working with is responsible for the final product that you will be using. However, in most cases, the person you are working with is selling a product that has been created by or used by the firm where they work. Often, the person selling that product has not done the due diligence to understand the "security risk" involved in purchasing a product. They trust that their firm has represented the investment fairly to them.

The Stanford Investment Firm was shut down by U.S. Marshals for lying to their clients. They also lied to their employees in order to sell more product. They sold international Certificates of Deposit that paid more interest than any other comparable product in the market. Those CDs also paid considerably more commission than other Certificates of Deposit. Most of their brokers trusted the firm and didn't ask the hard questions. Most of the clients trusted their broker and accepted vague answers to how that kind of yield was possible. Certainly, greed from both the brokers and the clients made it easier to accept the extra income without much scrutiny. Under the "trust, but verify" policy, it would be very difficult to buy something like that without verifying how it works.

Investors often get sucked into investment ideas because of the lure of large returns. The excitement of a big payoff can overcome a lot of concerns about how they are going to get those big returns. It is important to understand how an investment works and determine if it is good for you or just good for the guy selling it to you. It shouldn't be embarrassing and you shouldn't feel bad about asking the hard questions. The costs of being wrong are too great. It doesn't really matter how much you trust your guy, if he/she can't tell you how something works and why it works, you are better off waiting for something you can understand.

There is a lot to an investment that you need to know. How does it affect your taxes? How does it get its return? How does it protect my money? The most obvious example of how this can go wrong was the proliferation of derivative products that were sold as mortgage bonds. No one understood those products. Even the people that created the products themselves couldn't really explain them.

The fact that you may have trusted the people who were selling those to you didn't help you when they all began to unravel. If you had implemented the "trust, but verify" policy, you would have never allowed yourself to buy them in the first place. That would have been a very good thing in retrospect. Never feel bad about demanding to understand the investments you are going to use to secure your financial future. It's the least you should do.

RULE #21

A Market Is A Market Is A Market

"The pessimist complains about the wind, the optimist expects it to change, the realist adjusts the sails."
—**William Arthur Ward**

I remember learning this mantra during my first few months of training when I entered the investment business in 1985. My training group consisted of young bucks who were sure that we knew enough to take the investment world by storm. We spent most of our days pouring over the latest market news looking for the competitive edge we needed to rise to the top of a very tough business.

One day we were in class watching the equity markets fall. We had all been sure that the markets would rise. All of our best analysts believed they would rise. Our collectively brilliant minds believed that they would rise. Yet there we were, watching them fall. One of the big guns in my firm came in to speak to us after lunch that day. By reputation it was believed that he knew everything there was to know about the markets. Surely he could explain to us what had happened and how we could have been so wrong. That's when I heard the words that would stick with me for the rest of my career.

He shrugged and said, "A market is a market is a market."

We looked strangely at him and one of us said what all of us were thinking. "Huh?"

He chuckled and said, "It's pretty simple. A market is a market is a market. You can try to understand it. You can read every piece of financial news written, but at the end of the session, the price is going to be based on the collective feeling of those who have invested in or taken money out of the markets on any given day."

You will find that the day to day fluctuations of the markets really have very little to do with economics and have a lot to do with the fear or greed that guides the day to day decisions of people who are putting their money at risk at any given moment. Over the long run, the markets will tend to reflect their fair market value.

However, the vast majority of the time, the closing value will reflect a market that is either over-valued or under-valued. That is why it is so important to invest in the equity markets only if you have the time to wait out unreasonable market prices in the short-term. The markets don't reflect the events of a given day. They reflect the collective reaction to those events. I have always thought that a psychiatrist would have a better chance of predicting short-term market moves than would an economist.

The beauty of this rule is that once you understand it, you realize that the investment markets are pure and efficient and couldn't care less about how smart you are. That realization will force you to start thinking about the long-term, where your research might matter and where you should have been all along.

_____
_____
_____
_____
_____
_____
_____
_____
_____
_____
_____
_____
_____
_____
_____
_____
_____
_____
_____
_____
_____
_____
_____
_____
_____
_____
_____
_____

RULE #22

Inflation Can Kill You

---

*"Inflation is as violent as a mugger, as frightening as
an armed robber, and as deadly as a hit man."*

—Ronald Reagan

We haven't mentioned inflation yet, but it is known as the silent killer. It can eat away at a portfolio until much of the buying power is gone. Many investors don't think of themselves as risk takers. They want to make their money and then invest it in something that they perceive to be safe.

Over the years, I have seen hundreds of people who have come to me with a portfolio of Certificates of Deposit because they want to keep their money safe. If they have really given it some thought, they may be in a number of CDs that come due at different times. We call that a laddered portfolio. An investor may have some money in a one year CD, some in a three year CD, and some in a five year CD.

85

The thought behind that strategy is that when a CD comes due, the investor can take advantage of the higher rate for a longer-term CD because they are continually replacing the CD that came due with a CD at the end of the ladder. It is a good plan and it works well for those investors that need that kind of investment. The challenge comes in understanding what is really safe and what just appears to be safe.

Many investors believe that safety comes in the form of protecting your principal. That theory makes sense at first blush, but when you think about the long-term effect of inflation on a portfolio, things get a bit murky. Inflation is simply the increase in the cost of goods. Inflation doesn't affect the amount of money that you have, it affects the amount of goods and services you can buy with that money. The fact is that money isn't worth anything until you try to spend it. So the amount of goods and services that you can buy with a certain amount of money is critical to your financial success.

Think about it this way. If the cost of goods and services decreased by 50 percent and your portfolio decreased by 25 percent, that would be a great thing for you. The amount of things you could buy just increased considerably even though the amount of money you had decreased considerably. Money is only as good as what it can buy.

That's why it is important to protect your long-term money against the devastating effect of inflation. During my Certified Investment Management Analyst® designation training at the Wharton School of Business, I learned that fixed interest rate investments were safer than stocks in the short run. But after about ten years, that switched and stocks became a safer investment than bonds. By safer investment I mean that stocks would have less downside risk than bonds.

Stocks' overall risk is still higher, but most of that risk is upside risk and I have never heard a client complain about realizing upside risk. No one seems to mind making more money than they thought they would. On a yearly basis, stocks always have more downside risk, but even with that yearly volatility, stocks have a better chance of making money over longer periods of time because they can overcome the effect of inflation on your portfolio. Inflation is relentless. It eats away at the guaranteed rate of return that is so attractive in the bond market when interest rates are high.

It is important to understand the true meaning of safety before you implement it in your portfolio. You may have more risk than you think.

_____
_____
_____
_____
_____
_____
_____
_____
_____
_____
_____
_____
_____
_____
_____
_____
_____
_____
_____
_____
_____
_____
_____
_____
_____
_____
_____
_____

RULE #23

It's Never Too Good To Pass Up

*"Men in general are quick to believe that
which they wish to be true."*
—Julius Caesar

I remember my first venture into the world of private equity. The investment banking division of the firm I worked for had a deal that sounded great. Private equity is the part of the investment world that invests in new companies or companies that need money to grow. These are not companies that trade on an exchange. Your money is normally locked up for a long time with no easy way to get out.

Because they are so illiquid, private equity inherently has a lot of risk. But they also tend to be the best stories. The upside can be huge. The stories revolve around themes such as,

- "No one else is doing this!"

- "We have found a way to do this that will make everyone else in our industry obsolete!"
- "Remember what plastic did for the world economy? We are the new plastic!"

It is hard to keep from dreaming about what you might do with all that money when you hit it big. The problem is that the stories are someone else's dream. Dreams don't always come true, no matter how good they sound or how much you want them to succeed.

A friend of mine in the investment business gave me some good advice after a deal I liked didn't work out as well as I had hoped. He had about thirty years more experience than me.

He said, "Scott, you have to remember that all of these deals sound great. You can have ten deals that all sound equally good at the start. In my experience, four will go broke, four will break even, and two will hit it big. The key is to be in those two that hit it big. If you can't tell on the front end which two they are, then the only way to make money is to buy all ten deals."

His point is that big risk investments can really pay off, but in our business, the chance for big gains comes with an equal chance for big losses. You can't afford to simply count on guessing right the first time. The rest of his advice was even better.

He said, "Don't get sucked in by a good story. Good stories come by every day. Concentrate on the things you can control."

For me that is:

- Diversification: don't buy something your portfolio doesn't need just because it sounds good.
- Fundamentals: there is always a reason why this deal is different, but being different does not mean it is always better. Fundamentals work all the time.

- Costs: you can control costs and that can make as big a difference over time as anything else you do.
- Personal Finance: don't buy something you can't afford just because it sounds good. I know that it may appear that an investment may be able to save you, but those that can save you can also take you down.

I'm not saying that you should never invest in a good story. I'm just saying that they come around every day. When you do invest, make sure the rest of your bases are covered.

RULE #24

Improvise, Adapt, And Overcome

"Adapt or perish, now as ever, is nature's inexorable imperative."
—H. G. Wells

Improvise, adapt, and overcome. It is the unofficial slogan of the Marine Corps and was made popular by the Clint Eastwood movie, *Heartbreak Ridge*. The marines know something that should be self-evident to all of us: things go wrong a lot. Expect the unexpected. Don't be surprised when the best laid plans go awry. Don't spend a lot of time wishing things were different. Spend your time finding a solution.

You can plan for your retirement by forecasting an 8 percent return on your money for the next thirty years. You can figure out what you need to invest to make that plan work. And you can be very vigilant in implementing your plan. All of that doesn't really matter when we have a crisis like the one in 2008, The Great

Recession. You find that you are no longer close to meeting your retirement goal.

For instance, you invest for years to be able to buy a house on the lake and then one of your family members is in an accident and needs a lot of healthcare. So plans change. Things happen. In 2014 my house was hit by a tornado. I had seemed to be on a pretty good track with my investment goals. Then we had to focus on getting back in our home. For the benefit of my insurance advisor, who is my brother-in-law, I need to let you know that I had very good insurance, but that doesn't change the fact that my financial focus changed.

What do you do when things go wrong? I think most of us want to spend a lot of time talking about how we didn't deserve it or it just wasn't right. I have found that to be a waste of time. I am not saying that I don't participate, I just don't think it does much good.

Improvise. First you must look at your options. A lot of the people I know want to only look at the obvious options in front of them. The people I know that are successful tend to look outside the box for answers. Find creative ways to make your "new normal" work for you.

Adapt. You have to adapt to the changes in your life. The faster you begin to look at the world from your new perspective, the faster you find a solution to your challenges.

Overcome. Find a way to win. Goals change, plans change. It's your job to take the new circumstances and find a way to win.

When the World Trade Center came down on 9/11, our world changed in a lot of ways. Our nation had to improvise just to move forward, especially with the search and rescue. We had never seen anything like it before. We had to adapt to a world where this kind of thing was possible. A lot had to change, and we had to find a way to overcome. It was not acceptable to have this event define us. We needed to be defined by how we dealt with this event.

Over the years, I have spent time at the site watching crews dig us out of the hole of 9/11. Recently, I was there again to see the memorial and the pools created from the holes left from the World Trade Centers. It is inspiring to see something so beautiful come out of something so horrible. That is a grand reminder of how to improvise, adapt, and overcome.

This chapter is written with a great amount of respect for the Marine Corps and thanks for exemplifying the qualities that can be used by anyone to live a better life. Semper Fi.

RULE #25

Don't Take Short-Term Risk To Get Long-Term Results

"The biggest risk is not taking any risk...
In a world that's changing really quickly, the only strategy
that is guaranteed to fail is not taking risks."
—Mark Zuckerberg

Risk versus return. Investors hear about that all the time. There is no doubt that there is a high correlation between the risk you take and the expected return of the investment, but risk can be a hard thing to nail down. In the investment world, we talk about risk in most conversations as it deals with standard deviation.

Standard deviation is the amount of fluctuation in an investment. If an investment goes up 5 percent from its starting point during the year, and goes down 5 percent as well, its standard deviation for the year would be 10 percent. However, if it goes up

8 percent and goes down 2 percent, it still has a standard deviation of 10 percent, but the potential outcome seems to be more preferable. Standard deviation numbers will tell you how much an investment tends to fluctuate, but it doesn't tell you how much of that is up and how much is down. If there is more upside risk than downside risk, the chance of losing money decreases over time as the upside risk has a greater effect on the portfolio.

I have found that investors tend to use the standard deviation of an investment as a critical component of creating a portfolio. There is nothing wrong with that, but you have to consider other factors, such as the projected return of an investment, to give you a better idea of how the standard deviation effects your long-term results.

Look at the difference between fixed income and equities. There is no doubt that equities constitute a greater risk to your portfolio in any one year than does fixed income. On the surface, that looks good for fixed income, but with fixed income yielding a very low return, its low standard deviation is almost guaranteeing that the return won't overcome inflation. Inflation will eat up the buying power of the money your investments make over time.

On the equity side of things, the projected return on equities is much higher, but so is the projected risk. The equity markets have been up about 70 percent of the time over the past one hundred years and down about 30 percent of the time. People aren't really surprised when it rains if the weather report says the chance is at 30 percent. But over the years, you would expect a lot more sunny days than rainy.

The point is that the longer you hold an equity investment, the less chance that you lose some of your original investment and the greater your chance of beating inflation. The longer you hold a fixed income investment, the more risk you have of losing some of your original investment and the greater the chance that you will lose the battle with inflation.

Investors tend to look at the standard deviation of an investment over a year and use that to build a portfolio that should last for thirty years. In a class at the Wharton School of Business in the early 2000s, I was told that equities were actually a safer investment than bonds after about ten years. For a retirement plan or other long-term investments, that's a pretty good thing to know. Understanding the true risk of an investment can make a huge difference over time.

RULE #26

Gamify Your Portfolio

"My work is a game, a very serious game."
—M. C. Escher

When I was young, I used to travel with my dad when he would give speeches to various groups. He really didn't need me to tag along, but I was the fourth child and I think that by the time I came along, he probably got major points for getting me out of my mother's life for a bit.

One night, I was with my dad when he was giving a speech on a very serious topic, but often during the talk he would have the whole audience laughing. On the way home I asked him why he told jokes during such a serious speech. He explained that people don't have a very long attention span for serious subjects and adding some humor makes it easier for them to pay attention to the real subject.

He also said, "You don't always have to be serious just because you are dealing with a serious subject." I have always remembered that and it has served me well over the years. I am giving a lot of speeches around the country these days on investment ethics and the fiduciary standard debate. It really doesn't get much more boring than that for the average person. Adding humor has been a critical component in getting my message across on a subject that effects all investors.

Gamification is another branch of that same tree. Gamification is the idea of taking boring, hard, or unpleasant tasks and making them fun. The idea is to get paid in points for unpleasant tasks that need to be done and to use those points earned to pay for pleasant things. For example, you get points for taking out the trash and then you can apply those points to eat at your favorite restaurant. It sounds simple, but it really does work.

I first heard about gamification in the investment world about two years ago. A group was designing games for participants to play when investing money in their retirement plan. The result was that more people were putting more money in their retirement plan because the process had become enjoyable. You could get points for putting money in the plan and more points for meeting the company match.

Every week, I talk to people who say they just can't spare the money to invest. But those same people find the money to go out to dinner or buy expensive shoes. What they really mean is, "It's just not worth it to me to do this. It's not fun and I just can't see the benefit."

If you can find a way to make investing fun, you don't have to see the finish line in order to reach your goals. Investing is about what you do today to help achieve success in your future life. That is certainly a serious subject and not fun for most people.

Find ways to reward yourself for the hard things you have to do to be a successful investor. Work hard, reward yourself, have fun, and you will be amazed at what you can accomplish.

_____
_____
_____
_____
_____
_____
_____
_____
_____
_____
_____
_____
_____
_____
_____
_____
_____
_____
_____
_____
_____
_____
_____
_____
_____
_____
_____
_____
_____
_____

RULE #27

Past Performance Can Be An Indication Of Future Performance

"But many that are first will be last, and the last first."
—Matthew 19:30

A dvertisements in our business are required to say, "Past performance is no indication of future performance." Everyone sees that, but I don't think they really believe it. And they are not helped by the fact that a large number of advertisements spend an enormous amount of time talking about their past performance.

I compare that type of advertising to the shell game that magicians and street performers like to play. The shell is never where the people think it is. When investors ask the question, What can I make on this investment, the answer, I have no idea, would be correct. But it isn't what they want to hear. It is easy to find an

105

investment that has done exactly what investors want, show them past results, and talk them into investing with the hope that it will happen again.

The truth of the matter is that expecting an investment to keep outperforming is not reasonable. But that doesn't mean you can't look at past performance and gain some insight into the future. Although it is impossible to know exactly what an investment will do in the future, it is not that hard to determine an expected trend. Let me give you a few hints. "What comes up, must come down." "Once the pendulum swings far out to one side, it must come back."

The investment world is a reversion to the mean business. Good investments that do poorly should be expected to do well in the future. And the converse is true. Good businesses that have done exceptionally well recently will probably do poorly in the next cycle.

Now remember, I do not mean that the company itself is doing well or poorly. I mean their stock price is doing well or poorly. The price of a security rarely represents its exact intrinsic value. Investors are constantly loving it too much or hating it too much. Sooner or later, the truth will come out and the price trend will change.

That is the reason why Warren Buffett has often said that he spends a lot of time calculating the intrinsic value of a company. If an investor knows the intrinsic value and can wait until the market price dips significantly under that, he/she can buy a company with much less associated risk.

The truth is that past performance can be a pretty good indicator of future performance. It's just not what most people think. Many fund companies set their sights on the funds that have done really well and want you to believe that they will continue on that track for a long time. You never see an advertisement that says, "Our fund has been really poor the past few years but you should buy it now because it is going to turn around." Or, "Our fund has had a great run and it's probably going to go down for a while because investors are going to be taking some profits. You should probably get out now."

It doesn't take a rocket scientist to understand why investors want to buy into investments that have done well and sell those that haven't. It would just be nice if that ended up being the right move more often than it is.

RULE #28

Sometimes It's Just Not Your Fault

"Where I'm gonna beat him is in my mental mind!"
—Television interview with a boxer pre-fight, boxer unknown

I have always had a fascination with behavioral science. Some people are just interested in what people do, but I have always been interested in why people do. I took a class in nonverbal behavior in college. We called it Body Language. I have used what I learned in that class over and over again throughout my career. But the most interesting thing to me is not determining what someone's actions mean, but what they were thinking in the first place.

Most investors I talk with believe that successful investment advisors must know how to find better opportunities than other advisors. That seems reasonable, but I don't believe that is true. Finding good investment opportunities isn't that hard. The hard part is keeping your clients committed to the program. The secret to our success is the ability to consistently stop our clients from hurting themselves.

Why do smart people continually make bad decisions? Well, it just may not be their fault. Scientists have said for years that the medial prefrontal cortex of the brain is where you need to be to make good, long-term decisions. It is where you go to make linear, cognitive decisions, such as how to implement an investment plan. The problem is that your mind doesn't really access the medial prefrontal cortex very well when you are under emotional stress. It makes emotional decisions more from the amygdala. That part of the brain just wants to fix the problem at hand.

During the financial crisis of 2008, the Dow Jones plummeted to half its value and closed just above 6,400 on March 6, 2009. Any reasonable valuation of the market at that time would have told you that the Dow Jones Industrial Average was severely underpriced. When something is severely underpriced, most reasonable people would want to buy, but we spent a great deal of time talking our clients into holding the course and not selling.

Why would they want to sell something at a price much lower than its intrinsic value? I think most investors just couldn't get their medial prefrontal cortex to fire up and weigh in on the issue. Their emotional side was saying, "Stop the bleeding! You have to get out now and end this pain! I can't take this anymore!"

Studies by Dr. Martin Paulus of the University of California tell us that once the emotional side gets revved up, it can be almost impossible to shut it down and access the reasonable side of the brain.

What's most interesting to me is that there appears to be no relationship between being smart and making bad investment decisions. If you can't access the correct part of your brain for the decisions you need to make, then it is virtually impossible to make good decisions. How do you fix that problem? You better find someone who can. It is a strong argument for finding an advisor that you can trust to help you implement your process.

I know a lot of investors who feel like they are smart enough to do it on their own. I would say to those people, "Needing help doesn't mean you aren't smart enough. To the contrary, you are smart enough to know that you may not be able to make great decisions . . . and it just may not be your fault."

RULE #29

Expand Your Universe

*"Follow your bliss and the universe will
open doors where there were only walls."*
—Joseph Campbell

Imagine Captain Kirk has set off to look for other life forms in our universe. They have pulled away from space dock and he is just about to call for warp speed. He wants to get out there and see what he can find. Sulu is ready to hit the button when Spock says, "Wait, Jim, the company that created our software only has relationships with twenty-five planets. We aren't going to get to search the vast universe. We really need to stay in our own little part of space. If we hit warp speed now, we will end up too far into space."

"But Spock, our job is to look through all of space, not just a small part of space!"

"What can I say, Jim? It is not logical, but the software company gets paid by the planets to be part of their universe. If you don't pay, you don't play. We can't go outside the parameters they set or we won't have any backup."

"Okay, Sulu, set the *Enterprise* at cruising speed and I guess we will just float around and hope for the best."

That scenario is how the investment world works in a lot of cases. Many of the companies that sell product through a sales force, such as mutual fund companies, brokerages, banks, insurance companies, and investment banks, tend to want to put together a defined universe of investments that are allowed for their clients. Some may be products that are in-house, called proprietary products, and some are simply groups that were put together for a specific purpose.

The challenge comes when the products that you are using aren't the best for you. It becomes very awkward for your "advisor" to recommend selling what you have and buying someone else's product. That would be similar to walking up to your boss and saying, "I've looked at all of the people out there that do what I do and I just don't think I am the best at what I do. I think you need to fire me and hire somebody better." That is just not a conversation you hear much in the workplace. It is also not a conversation you hear much in the investment world.

The onus is on you to make sure that you are either willing to spend the time to assure your investments are behaving properly or have an advisor that is using an "open architecture" platform. Open architecture means that you are not prohibited from buying any investment vehicle that makes sense for your portfolio. If you have that kind of platform, you will have taken a big step in overcoming a conflict of interest that occurs all too often in the investment world.

Of course, the easiest way to avoid that trap is to use someone whose financial interests are not tied to the investments they use. That is still a relatively low percentage of the people working as advisors in the United States. Many firms, regardless of how they are compensated, are coming up with open architecture platforms for their salesforce to use. Try to find one that includes passive investments, such as index funds. Expand your universe and watch the stars line up in your favor. "Kirk out."

RULE #30

Passive Almost Always Beats Active

'The stock market serves as a relocation center at which money is moved from the active to the patient."
—**Warren Buffett**

On the surface, actively managed investments make a lot of sense. Investors are reassured that they have someone smart at the helm plodding into work every day just to make sure that they are doing better than average. Surely a really smart person who has dedicated their life to understanding how to make more money than the average guy would be a good person to have in your corner.

It's a very good argument. If only there were more evidence to prove that to be true! Unfortunately, Dr. Eugene Fama won the Nobel Prize for Economics mostly by providing evidence to the contrary.

Dr. Fama's work is readily available if you want to drill down deeper, but the CliffsNotes™ of his findings are as follows. He found that active managers who consistently beat their corresponding index over long periods of time do exist, which is the good news. The bad news is that only about 2 percent of active managers can beat their average and overcome the extra fees they charge over a long period of time. More bad news is that it takes approximately thirty-seven years to know for sure if a manager is good or if he/she is just lucky. If Dr. Fama's research is true, then investors are spending an enormous amount of time looking for the rarest of rare gems.

It's not so hard to understand. In order to be better, you have to be different. You have to take bigger risks. Investors don't like different or increased risk when it doesn't pay off. In order to keep investors in your fund, you can't spend a lot of time looking worse than your index. The only way to protect your fund from that is to look a lot like the index you are compared to. If you do that, your returns will look a lot like the index as well.

So why are investors willing to pay more for a manager that is going to look a lot like an index fund that costs a lot less? Most actively managed funds spend a lot of money on marketing to tell you how they are going to do better, and they are very believable. We also know from Rule #3 that most of the advisors in the investment business are paid by the products they sell. Index funds typically don't pay anything to anyone.

If you get paid by the product, and index funds don't pay anything, it is easy to see why those advisors working on a commission wouldn't offer index funds as an option. Quite the contrary, they will spend a lot of time telling you why active management is the way to go. The tide is changing as the evidence grows in support of passive management.

That being said, I am not saying that there is no place for active managers. The peace of mind that someone is actually watching what is going on in your portfolio and has the responsibility to make changes on your behalf may stop many investors from making big mistakes and big mistakes are a great thing to avoid. There is always the chance that you will find one of the treasured 2 percent that are just great. I'm just saying that you should think hard about why you would pay up for something so hard to get.

RULE #31

The Years Teach Much That The Days Will Never Know

"Life can only be understood backwards;
but it must be lived forwards."
—Søren Kierkegaard

My father has a lot of quotes about life. One of his favorite quotes is, "The years teach much that the days will never know." Now when I was a kid, I had a hard time understanding exactly what that meant. But the more the years go by the more I understand the quote. It's not so unlike, "I can't see the forest for the trees." People get caught up in their daily lives and those daily life details become what is most important to them.

Both of my daughters recently played in a tennis tournament. As I watched them I thought about how far they had come and how positive the tennis tournament had been for them. They both

121

lost tough matches that they thought they should have won and were pretty sad about how things turned out. I told them that ten years from now, they wouldn't remember their matches on a Saturday afternoon in February.

One day they may look back and think about how they became good tennis players. They may remember all the hard work and practice, but there wouldn't be one match or one tournament that made all the difference. It would be years of matches and tournaments. It would be years of practice. What would make the difference is continually doing the right things no matter the result of any one day.

In the investment world, it is just as hard to look past the day to day performance of your investments and continue to keep your sight focused on the master plan. Every day, the financial press will bombard you with information about what is happening right now and why that information should make a difference in your life. But that is rarely true. What happens today is very significant if you are going to need all of your money tomorrow, but if you are preparing for the future (education of your children, retirement, legacy), then today is usually just a blip on the radar screen.

Investors are at a disadvantage because it is natural to look at what is going on now and become emotional about what that might do to your future. And, as we know from Rule #28, emotion is not a good quality in investing. Fear and greed are the two things that great investors take advantage of to create superior results. It's not the other way around.

There are certain things that you have to do to become a great tennis player. None of those things involve winning a lot of matches as you are learning the game. But there is a mound of evidence that you will win a lot of matches if you continue to do the right things and don't let today's result shift you from your path.

My business partner of thirty years says, "There is no way to get experience except through time."

Somewhere down the road, if you stay the course, you will understand why your results today have so little to do with your results twenty years from now. It is the effort today that will matter down the road. Until then, I would suggest that you base your decisions on years of history and evidence more so than how you feel in the moment.

RULE #32

This Ain't Rocket Science

*"The key is taking responsibility and initiative,
deciding what your life is about and prioritizing your life
around the most important things."*
—Stephen Covey

I have been in the financial industry a long time. It seems to me that a lot of investors think that they have to be smarter than everyone else in order to win. They forget that investing isn't a game against everyone else. It is a game against yourself. You are the one who makes the money that you can invest. You are the one who wants to buy the new 64-inch flat screen with Blu-ray instead of putting more money into a college fund. You are the one who sets long-term goals and then has to implement the plan that will get you there.

On a football field, everyone has the same goal. You need to have a higher score at the end of the game than the other guy. It doesn't matter how high the score is as long as it is higher. A win is a win . . . period.

In the investing world, everyone has a different goal. Some people put more of their own money toward reaching their goals. Some people have easier goals than others. Comparing your own situation to everyone else's situation can give you a very lopsided view of how you are doing.

This idea of competing is perpetuated in the financial media every day. Experts talk about all the winners and losers of the day, the week, or the month. Trying to keep up with all of that stuff will drive you crazy and make you do things that are not in your best interest. Rule #6 is "Investing is hard." Investing is hard, but not for the reasons you might think. It is emotionally grueling. It is a contrary activity that begs you to do the wrong thing at the wrong time. It wants you to believe that unimportant things are much more important than they truly are.

The hard part is understanding what is important and sticking to your beliefs while being bombarded with information that makes you want to question those beliefs. There are some things that I have come to believe over the years that have helped me stay the course with my clients, as well as my own portfolio.

- The stock market becomes less risky over time and the bond market becomes riskier.
- How your money is allocated between assets classes is much more critical to your success than finding the next great money manager.
- Diversification is key to a long-term strategy.
- Paying attention to your portfolio every day is seldom a good thing.
- You have to know your time horizon and act accordingly.

- You have to hold your advisors accountable for what they are doing.
- Costs matter a lot and are not always easy to understand.

It is important to note that you should not hold advisors accountable for your return. You should hold them accountable for how they got your return. Returns are arbitrary numbers, but the process applied to get those returns needs to fit your goals.

It's not about being smarter than anyone else or finding the silver bullet that will change your life. To use another football analogy, it is about blocking and tackling. You will be surprised at how good your running backs and receivers look when your offensive line knows how to block.

It ain't rocket science. It's simple principles, consistently implemented by an investor who is committed to the process.

RULE #33

Invest In A Roped Off Sea

"Don't ever take a fence down until you know why it was put up."
—**Robert Frost**

Jimmy Buffett is one of my favorite songwriters. He can write a short novel in three verses and a chorus that takes three and a half minutes to sing. He has a song entitled "There's a Cowboy in the Jungle." It's about a cowboy who gets stuck on an island and doesn't have the money to leave so he hangs out with the sailors and the tourists.

Part of the lyrics talk about how the cowboy doesn't want to swim in a "roped off sea." His reference to a roped off sea comes, I think, from the fact that on beaches around the world where there are problems with sharks, the local authority will rope off part of the ocean with netting so the sharks can't get in that area.

That process makes it safe for the swimmers. I saw a lot of that when I was in Australia. You weren't required to swim in that roped area, but it was safe. You would see a lot of families in the roped off areas because no one wanted to take the chance of letting their children swim where there were no ropes.

Of course, the surfers couldn't surf there, the kayakers couldn't paddle there, and the young adults that wanted to get away from the families would venture off to the un-roped areas. There were a lot of reasons why someone would want to swim in the un-roped part of the ocean. But those who were responsible for the safety of someone who they cared for stayed inside the ropes.

Investing is not much different. If you are investing money for something that is important to you, then you need to set parameters. Those parameters are called your Investment Policy Statement, and everyone needs one. Your Investment Policy Statement is created at a time when you can think rationally. It doesn't have to do with what you may like today. It has to do with what you think is an appropriate way to invest over the long run. It keeps your investments away from the sharks.

Investment Policy Statements are not rigid. They can change over time as you change. But they are there to make sure that you don't go over the fence and swim in the open water just because you feel good on a certain day. It's one thing to take risk personally, but it's a whole different thing when you decide to take risk that affects your family and those who are precious to you.

Those investments that have to be there for college, for retirement, and for life, should be invested using an Investment Policy Statement. There are a lot of good resources to guide you through the process.

For those investments that you don't mind losing, feel free to swim outside the ropes and hope for the best. As the Australians say, "Good on ya, mate."

RULE #34

Old School Still Works

"What people don't realize is that professionals are sensational because of the fundamentals."

—Barry Larkin

I was driving to our regional mall last week. It is not something I usually do by choice. I am a downtown shopping kind of guy. I remember Yogi Berra once saying, "Nobody goes to Coney Island anymore; there are too many people there." That's how I feel about the mall. You can't avoid the traffic.

I know that you folks who live in the big cities won't shed too many tears for me, but for a guy who can drive to work during rush hour in about four minutes, traffic at the mall is horrible. I was behind a person at one stop light who wouldn't move after the light changed. Finally, when I honked, he looked up from his phone and moved along. I changed lanes and got behind a person going eight miles an hour while looking down at her phone. I couldn't change lanes so I stayed there as she approached the next light. The light turned red, but that didn't really stop her as she stared at her phone and continued through the light at the lightning pace of eight miles per hour.

Recently I met my wife at a restaurant. When I sat down she was looking at her phone and said that a number of people on her Facebook page were debating the terrible news about the market. It appeared to be about the Fed's possible reaction to the new jobs report. This is news that many of us have speculated about for months, but the news media decided that yesterday was a good time to break that news to all the people out there who wait to see it on their smartphones. This wasn't new news, it was old news, rehashed.

In the old days, there was a big advantage to being one of the first to get and analyze market news. There was limited access to the markets and you could make money by beating others to the punch. Nowadays, news is immediate and it comes not by subscription to the *Wall Street Journal*, but to our smartphones while we drive eight miles an hour down a busy road. It doesn't make sense to spend so much time trying to beat others to the market with news that is being processed by the entire country at the same time.

So, what does the smart money do? I think the smart money has had to retreat to basic investment philosophy. It has had to keep its vision focused firmly on the horizon and not at the day to day commentary that is becoming more and more useless as the playing field becomes more and more level.

Even though much has changed over the years, the fundamentals of investment philosophy have remained the same since Benjamin Graham wrote his definitive book, *The Intelligent Investor*. It is still worth reading. It is old school and old school still works.

RULE #35

Never Assume

"People who jump to conclusions rarely alight on them."
—Philip Guedalla

Assumptions can get you in a lot of trouble. We make them all the time. We assume the run-down looking person in ragged clothes is a bad person and the guy in the three-piece suit is a good man. Of course, it is possible that the run-down looking person in ragged clothes works for a local charity and has devoted his life to helping others. It is also possible that the guy in the three-piece suit is Bernie Madoff. You never know. Never knowing is the problem with assumptions. By the time you find out if you are right, you may have made a big mistake.

In the world of investments, it is very easy to jump to conclusions. It is easy to assume how the markets will react to news, good or bad. But the markets don't jump to conclusions. The markets are an immediate reflection of the consensus view of the world

137

on a second-to-second, minute-to-minute basis. The problem is that most people vote in the markets with very little information. The markets reflect assumptions that are made based on limited information by people who are motivated by fear and greed. That doesn't seem to be a great recipe for success in a long-term investment strategy.

To make matters worse, you can turn on the TV any day and hear very smart people taking completely different sides of an issue, and they both sound right. They make you believe that you need to take action now if you ever want to retire and live the good life.

So what is an investor supposed to do? Investors are supposed to never assume that they know more than the collective markets. They are supposed to never assume that they are faster, smarter, or have found the silver bullet that will take them to the top of the investing pyramid. They are supposed to use empirical evidence to make decisions based on well-published facts and investment theory and understand that today is not a new paradigm. Today is not the day that you know more than anyone else.

What makes this so hard is that news flashes and top stories get you all excited and make you feel like you need to do something *now*. The only way to do that is to start making assumptions about things before all the facts come out.

To do it right, you have to take a breath and review your Investment Policy Statement that you wrote after reading Rule #33. Take time to remember how you said you wanted to invest before you got all excited and stay the course you set for yourself when you were thinking more clearly.

In the old days, there were people who legally got the news before the rest of us. The markets were much less efficient and there were barriers to entry in the investment world that created opportunity. Those days are gone in the traditional markets that most of us invest in, but if you have the time, use solid investment theory, and base your decisions on the facts and not your personal feelings, the investment world can still make your dreams come true.

RULE #36

There Is Always A Market

"Price is what you pay. Value is what you get."
—Warren Buffett

Understanding how a market works is not hard. Some people want to make money and decide to buy into the market, while others have already made or lost money and want to get out. Although now almost everything is done by computer, in the old days there was a floor broker who facilitated those trades. There is still a middle man or middle computer who facilitates those trades. Those middle men facilitated, on average, over thirty-eight million trades a day in 2022 just on the New York Stock Exchange. With that kind of volume representing millions and millions of stockholders, it is very hard to believe that you would have a hard time finding a buyer and a seller when you needed to sell.

There will always be a market, but at what price? That is tricky part.

On a day to day basis the markets move based on emotion. If the market is rising and people in the market are making money, then those who are not in the market want to buy in so they can make money too. So, prices rise. If the market is falling and people are losing money, investors want to get out and stop the pain. So the prices decline.

It is understandable that those who are not in the market have a hard time investing when they see everyone else getting out. They stay on the sidelines until they feel okay to invest. This kind of behavior is what starts trends. The average investor can ride those trends for an uncomfortable length of time. It is called herd mentality, and being part of the herd can get you in a lot of trouble when investing. You want to make money like the others, so you buy into a high market. You want to avoid losses like your friends, so you get out of a down-market.

It is easy to see why people act that way. But just because it is easy to understand doesn't make it right. On the contrary, the people that go against the herd tend to do quite well over time. This is called buying low and selling high. Everyone wants to do it, but it is difficult to accomplish. All of your emotions are telling you to do the wrong thing at the wrong time, and you are required to look past your feelings and do the right thing.

For years, we in the business have looked at contra indicators to tell us what to do. Contra indicators tell you one thing, but mean something else. Herd mentality is a contra indicator. When everyone is buying, that can be a sell signal. When everyone is selling, that can be a buy signal. Forcing yourself to go against the herd has been a very profitable exercise for a long time.

I remember the market crash of 1987 when the Dow Jones Industrial Average dropped over 600 points in a day and closed down 508 points lower than the previous day. That was, at the time, the biggest one-day drop in history. The big story was the next day when the markets opened down again and it looked like we could be in for another record setting day to the down side.

Computer trading programs were triggered to automatically sell stock if the last trade was lower. As the market crashed, there was a void of buyers. The Dow fell another 200 points right at the open before a group of about six buyers decided to go against the enormous pressure to follow the herd. They decided to bet on a market rebound by buying some call options on the Dow Jones Industrial Average. A relatively small investment of about $35,000 filled the void of buyers and the next trade ticked up instead of down. That uptick in the market triggered a computer buy program that began buying stock, which triggered another and another buy program. That one small move triggered computer trading programs to begin buying and the Dow rocketed back up.

There is always someone that will take the other side of a trade. The price may have to change in order to find a willing buyer or seller, but they are out there.

In early 2009, as the equity markets continued to drop, a reader asked me, "What if the Dow goes to zero?" He was serious and he was scared. I told him that the Dow has never been at zero. The first day the Dow Jones Industrial Average began to trade, it opened around seven.

Companies have intrinsic value and as long as that is true, there will always be a market. The key to success is to know when to buy and when to sell. Often, it is when the crowd is doing just the opposite.

RULE #37

Volatility Is Good

"Never think that lack of variability is stability.
Don't confuse lack of volatility with stability, ever."
—Nassim Nicholas

My daughters are tennis players. They both hit their first balls when they were young, around four years old. Hitting balls for fun is one thing, but in recent years they have both decided to play more competitive tennis.

Both are on their high school tennis team, the oldest on varsity and the youngest on junior varsity. A lot of people say that winning is everything in competitive sports, but I don't think that is true. If you are winning at everything, you aren't really getting better, are you? In order to get better, you have to play better competition. You can't do that and win all the time.

I am excited when they are able to lose and then tell me what happened and what they learned from it. Then I know they are growing and getting better. There is only one number one player in the world. The rest of us are apt to lose at any time. Even more importantly, I think, is the fact that losing makes you appreciate winning so much more. The thrill of victory is so much sweeter when you know the agony of defeat.

The point is that the downside of things often serves a great purpose in your pursuit of success. It is no different in the investment world.

Volatility is a good thing. It is the only thing that provides us with the opportunity to succeed. The idea that your investments would go up every year is a nice thought, but it doesn't work in practice or in theory. Markets are created by bringing buyers and sellers together. The buyers think that prices are too low at the same time that the sellers think prices are too high.

If the markets were to go up every year, then there would be no reason to sell for most owners of securities. If there were no sellers, there would be no market. Down-markets provide opportunities for investors just as up markets provide opportunities. Greed and fear, the two biggest drivers of market movements, can only exist in a volatile environment.

A critical key to success in the investment world is to embrace and understand the volatility of the markets and then use it to your advantage. That is easier said than done, but just because it is hard doesn't make it less true. A faith in the majority to be consistently wrong and force markets to move more than they should, can bode well for the patient methodical investor. A healthy dose of fear in an upmarket and greed in a down-market can be a very good thing for your investment portfolio, even though your heart wants to do just the opposite.

Ben Hogan, the golf legend, once said, "If your golf swing feels good, you are most likely doing something wrong."

The same can be said about investing. Even though most of the investors I talk with would prefer a sure and consistent thing, the better route is to embrace the volatility, understand it, and use it to your advantage.

_____
_____
_____
_____
_____
_____
_____
_____
_____
_____
_____
_____
_____
_____
_____
_____
_____
_____
_____
_____
_____
_____
_____
_____
_____
_____
_____
_____

RULE #38

Discipline Is Rewarded

*"We must all suffer one of two things: the pain of discipline
or the pain of regret and disappointment."*

—Jim Rohn

lvis was asked in an interview in 1958, "How does it feel to be
an overnight success?"

Elvis answered, "It feels like a heck of a long night." Of
course, it had been years since Elvis had gone into Sun Records to
record a song for his mother. He had been traveling the Louisiana
Hay Ride Circuit and played anywhere someone would have him.
Then it all hit the nation at the same time and he looked like an
overnight success.

Lou Holtz said to me once, (well, it was actually me and 200
other people in the room), "It's funny how those that work the
hardest seem to be the luckiest." On *The Today Show* recently,
they were talking about how Mark Zuckerberg works fifty to sixty

hours a week directly in his job, but that he spends his whole life trying to make Facebook better.

I know that there are exceptions. There is the person at the slot machine that wins ten million dollars or that guy who invented the Pet Rock. Sometimes you just fall into a win, but those times are few and far between.

For the 99 percent of us who have to earn what we have, discipline is the foundation for success. It is one thing to want it and something completely different to go out and get it.

Archie Manning said that he would go out to the practice field with Peyton, Eli, and Cooper at five in the morning and work on their football skills. There is no doubt that they had good genes, but good genes isn't enough. The discipline to do what you have to do, especially when you would rather be doing something else, is what gets you across the finish line first.

Investing is no different. You have to have a disciplined approach. If you wander around the investment world changing your strategy often and simply hoping something will work out, it probably won't. Even the high-risk investment strategies demand discipline. It takes great discipline to see the down side of a strategy and continue to stick with it until you recognize the upside. In order to do that, you must understand the strategy you are implementing and you must have confidence that it will work. If you don't have that, you will make mistakes . . . sometimes over and over again.

Jim Parker, in his piece "Living with Volatility, Again," stated, "The market volatility is worrisome, no doubt. But through discipline, diversification, and understanding how the markets work, the ride can be made bearable. At some point, value re-emerges, risk appetites re-awaken, and for those who acknowledged their emotions without acting on them, relief replaces anxiety."

It is the discipline to learn about what you are doing, the discipline to create a proper investment strategy, and the discipline to implement that strategy correctly that will make the difference in your investment life. If you can't do that yourself, then you need the discipline to hire an expert to do it for you. If you can get that right, then you will be well on your way to a financial overnight success.

_____
_____
_____
_____
_____
_____
_____
_____
_____
_____
_____
_____
_____
_____
_____
_____
_____
_____
_____
_____
_____
_____
_____
_____
_____
_____
_____
_____
_____
_____

RULE #39

When You've Won, Stop Playing

---

*"If you're playing a poker game and you look around the table
and can't tell who the sucker is, it's you."*
—Paul Newman

Most of us realize that investing is not a game. It is more serious than a game. The consequences are too great to treat
it as such, but you do keep score. Every month you get a
statement that tells you how your account performed. It is inevita-
ble that you will feel that you have either won or lost that month
based on your investment return.

There are a lot of variables to consider when deciding how well
you are reaching your goals. Inflation rates, raises at work, college
scholarships . . . the list goes on and on. Nevertheless, each month
you give yourself a grade.

You may remember Rule #26, Gamify Your Investments. The
right kinds of games can make investing more fun and more prof-

itable. The problem comes from not knowing when the game is over. This chapter could have just as easily been titled, Don't Stop Playing Until You've Won. On the one hand, I have seen people retire from their job at sixty-five and want to change their portfolio to all fixed income because they have retired. Most sixty-five-year-olds still have a quarter of a century to go before they see their Maker, but they are investing as if they may die any day. They may be done with work, but their investment portfolio still has a lot of work to do.

On the other hand, investors who have taken risks all their lives tend to want to take those risks long after the need has diminished. I remember an eighty-year-old couple that once met with me. Ninety percent of their portfolio was in equities and most of that was in one stock. That one stock was the stock of the company he used to work for. He had bought it over the years and it was the main reason that he had made enough money to retire.

I asked him, "If you started today with all cash, would you buy that much stock in that company?" He, of course, said no. I asked him, "If that stock doubled, would it change your life?"

He said no. He said that they didn't have any big purchases or big trips to take. He really didn't need a lot more money.

I asked him, "If that stock lost half its value, would it change your life?"

He said, "Of course it would! We would have to change a lot of things we do now if that happened."

Then why on earth would they keep taking that kind of risk? It is risky to have that much of your worth tied up in any one investment. When you have won, stop playing! You don't have to look far to find out what I mean. Worldcom. Enron. Both were big companies that looked solid . . . until they weren't. And keeping an eye on your risk profile is on you. I don't mean that you need to stop investing, just stop playing the game you have been playing and start another one that is more appropriate.

Investment advisors have become very good at determining the maximum amount of risk an investor can stand and then forcing them to accept that risk for the rest of their life. It shouldn't be that way.

Know what game you should be playing and when you have won, stop and start a new, more appropriate game.

_____

_____

_____

_____

_____

_____

_____

_____

_____

_____

_____

_____

_____

_____

_____

_____

_____

_____

_____

_____

_____

_____

_____

_____

_____

_____

_____

_____

_____

_____

RULE #40

There Is No Free Ride

"We must explain the truth: There is no free lunch."
—Grace Napolitano

I like country music. No genre tells a story quite like country music. There is a song that talks about guys trying hard to make a living. It's by Jason Aldean and it is called "That's the Only Way I Know". In the song they talk about farming. One verse states the importance of learning that you only get what you earn. What a great lesson!

You may think that your boss owes you more than you are getting or that your friends aren't pulling their weight in some matter. But dirt, as Jason Aldean called it, doesn't have emotions. It doesn't mistreat you. It simply is what it is. If you don't pull your weight by disking, planting, watering, and harvesting your crops, your crops will suffer. You can't say that it is anybody's fault but your own. That's on you.

I understand that there are a lot of outside forces that determine how well you do, but you don't have a chance if you don't put in the effort to do your part. That's why the song goes on to stress the importance of focusing on what you can control. No matter what happens to those crops, you still have to put in the work if you want to have a chance.

The investment world is the same way. It is so easy to take shortcuts. There is always someone who will tell you how they can get you there faster, with less effort, and with less financial commitment. I have found that even though there are exceptions (some people really do win the lottery), shortcuts virtually never work.

I know that it hurts to give up things you want today for things you may want tomorrow, but sacrificial giving doesn't just work at church. It works in most things that really matter. If you want to have the money to send your children to college or enjoy retirement with your spouse, then you have to find out what it will take to get you there.

That means that you have to have reasonable expectations. Make decisions based on accurate data, not wishful thinking. Once you see what you have to do, then you have to go out and make it happen. As the old joke goes, "It's not rocket surgery!"

Develop a plan. Work hard to implement your plan. And as they say in farming, "God willing and the creek don't rise, you'll get where you want to go."

In the words of my great friend, Dr. Gordon Grant, "Ever onward."

_____
_____
_____
_____
_____
_____
_____
_____
_____
_____
_____
_____
_____
_____
_____
_____
_____
_____
_____
_____
_____
_____
_____
_____
_____
_____
_____
_____
_____
_____

RULE #41

Speed Is Not Your Friend

"My fear is that faster and easier ways of investing will allow people to lose more money faster and easier"

—David Booth, Chairman and Founder of Dimensional Fund Advisors

We are a society that wants to go faster. We want faster planes, trains, and automobiles. We want faster Internet, faster cable, faster everything. But if you are an investor you don't want everyone to be faster, just you.

You know the joke about the two hikers in the woods that came upon some very fresh bear sign? One of the hikers took his pack off, got out his running shoes, and started changing from his hiking boots. The other hiker laughed at him and said, "You can't outrun a bear!" The hiker, now in his running shoes, said, "I don't have to outrun the bear. I just have to outrun you."

When I first started in the investment world in 1985, I worked for the second oldest member firm of the New York Stock

Exchange, which was a big deal. You couldn't buy stock on the New York Stock Exchange if you didn't go through a member firm. Access was huge. But it also provided me with something even more valuable.

I was plugged into the information system, and I was able to get information on stocks as soon as it became public. Most people had to wait for news to be published in the newspaper or on television, and they rarely broke into regular scheduled programming to give you daily stock market news. I could use that news to my advantage.

Not anymore. Now that we have cell phones at 5G service and apps that will automatically alert you to any news anywhere, the advantage of time has gone away. If something happens in the stock market at 2:06 p.m., everyone who cares at all would know it by 2:07.

Speed has taken away a great advantage. What we are left with is a market where everyone is reacting to news at the same time. The more speed, the more efficient the markets become. And the exchanges that trade stocks and bonds are some of the most efficient machines in the world.

It is no longer reasonable to think that someone has the inside scoop on something. And if that is true, then what does an investor do? The first thing is to ignore all of those pundits on the financial news that act like they do. Secondly, realize that short-term market plays are guesses just like the craps table at a casino. The short-term market is moved by the collective emotions of buyers and sellers at a moment in time, and that is almost impossible to figure out. Thirdly, if you want to use your financial skills to grow your investments, think long-term. In the long-term, financials still matter.

Take a breath and slow down. Save your speed for the Internet. And be okay with the idea that you are not smarter than the markets at any one moment in time. There are a lot of proven ways to be better than the average investor over time, and none of them involve speed.

RULE #42

Pick A Process Before You Pick A Partner

*"The reason most major goals are not achieved is that
we spend our time doing the second thing first."*
—**Robert J. McKain**

In the world of investments, it seems to me that way too often investors pick a professional to work with before they pick a process. Without defining the process, everyone looks like they do the same thing. So, your choice is based not on your needs, but on the investment world version of a beauty contest. Who do you know? Who do you know that knows someone? Who has good advertisements? Who seems smart, ethical, successful? Those are all good qualities, and I would encourage you to find someone that has those qualities . . . but not until you decide what kind of relationship you want first.

I have a good friend who is a great doctor that I used for my knee replacement years ago. I also have a good friend who is a great doctor that I used for some throat surgery a few years ago. Both are good people. Both have great reputations. Both are exceptional surgeons. I would have never considered using my throat surgeon for my knee surgery, and I certainly wouldn't have used my knee surgeon for my throat surgery. The fact is that neither one of those doctors would have let me use them inappropriately either.

That is not the way it works with investments. In the investment world everyone tends to look the same, but they are not. The vast majority of investment professionals in the brokerage, insurance, and banking business get paid by the companies that created the product they use. The payout can vary greatly from product to product.

Investment product companies tend to pay more for new products just coming to market or old products that have lost their glitter. They pay more for the things they need to sell and less for the things they don't. Nothing about that process shouts, "What's best for the client?" The fiduciary side pays the same for every investment . . . zero.

When you get paid nothing for everything, it is much easier to make a choice on behalf of your client. When you have to choose between your client suffering by not getting the best product or you suffering because what the client needs doesn't pay you very much money, it gets pretty hard to be objective. When a commission-based investment professional hasn't done very well in a particular month, their parents are in a nursing home, and their kids are in college . . . well, you can see how hard it might be to sell you something with a low paying commission.

That being said, I still think a lot of investors need that kind of relationship. The fiduciary adviser does not go out seeking the hottest new investment ideas. They don't work around the fringes of the investment product world. They stay safe because they have a fiduciary responsibility to make sure you don't invest in something that might be too risky. So, how does an investor decide what kind of relationship they need?

For me it is pretty simple. Are you the kind of investor that likes to be in control of your choices? Do you want to be the captain of your own fate? Do you want investment professionals to pitch you ideas and then you decide what you want to buy? Then you don't need a fiduciary. A fiduciary relationship would just make you miserable. You need someone that gets paid by the product and has access to all the investment sizzle out there. It will be up to you to know how much you are paying for the products you buy, and it will be up to you to decide what you need.

Do you want to spend your time at work or in retirement doing the things that you do best? Do you need someone to do the heavy lifting for you with your investments? Would you prefer not to have to look over the shoulder of your investment professional and constantly worry if you are in the right investments? Then you need someone that has a legal responsibility to do what is in your best interest. You need someone who has the discretion to make decisions on a day to day basis on your behalf without having to bother you every time they want or need to make a trade. You need a fiduciary.

The problem is that investors so often don't narrow down the field to those that do what they need before they make a choice of who to work with. If you do the first thing first, it can make all the difference in the world. It is perfectly fine to pick someone you really like, who has great commercials, or who your friends have recommended, just as long as they actually do what you need them to do. Once you pick a process, let the beauty contest begin.

RULE #43

Let The Market Come To You

"Because nobody wants to get rich slowly."
—Warren Buffett

Warren Buffett was famously asked once, "Why can't other people do what you do?" His answer made my rule quote for Rule #43, "Because nobody wants to get rich slowly." I have almost spent four decades in the investment business and I can tell you that has been my experience as well. Investors feel that they have to find a way to beat the markets. They look for advisors that they feel can beat the markets. Everyone talks about beating the index and outperforming their peers.

What Warren realized in his teens that made him a billionaire in his 70s was that you don't have to beat the markets, you just have to let the markets do their thing and make sure that you are there when it happens.

There are thousands of investment professionals that wake up every day looking for a way to achieve outperformance. There are millions of investors that believe that if they try hard enough, they can find the silver bullet and get rich quick. I am not against that idea, but my challenge is in finding any evidence that people can do that consistently. Can someone do it? Absolutely. Will someone win the lottery? Absolutely. Can normal people repeat that process with the expectation that they can do it too? I haven't been able to find evidence of that.

You have to take enormous risks to get rich quickly and there is nothing better than realizing upside risk and nothing worse than realizing downside risk. When you consider the fact that you not only have to pick the right investment to buy to win that game, you also have to successfully know when to sell it, it becomes easier to see why it is mostly a loser's game. In order to win you have to get it right twice, but to lose you only have to be wrong once.

What Warren knew was that the markets will give you what you need if you just let them come to you instead of trying to beat them. He also knew that you have to be patient and give them time to do their thing. Markets can work against you for an uncomfortable amount of time. Markets will beg you to do the wrong thing at the wrong time. But investors who are patient have always been able to count on the consistency of returns over the past hundred years. Equities have given investors about 10 percent a year. Bonds have given investors around 5 percent per year. And money markets have given investors about nothing if you mark it against inflation.

This has been true no matter what has happened in the world. We were an agricultural society in the early 1900s. Then we were an industrial society, a technology society, and now a service society. Through it all the free market system has averaged about 10 percent. The key is to not pick the winners but to own the whole market. If you pick the winners, you may be wrong. The one thing we know is that, over time, there will be a lot of winners and losers. It is virtually impossible to know which is which. So, you own it all. You accept the fact that you will own the losers because that also means that you will own the winners. And that is how you get 10 percent in equities over a long period of time.

Then all you have to do is math. Ten percent a year will double your money in 7.2 years. The earlier you start the more you will have. It is not sexy. It is not exciting. But it is this easiest way I know to get rich . . . slowly. Just let the market come to you. And if you are patient enough, you can do all kinds of exciting things with all the money you make.

_____
_____
_____
_____
_____
_____
_____
_____
_____
_____
_____
_____
_____
_____
_____
_____
_____
_____
_____
_____
_____
_____
_____
_____
_____
_____
_____
_____
_____

RULE #44

Put Your Money In Buckets

"You are the chief bucket filler, and the best way to fill buckets is with excellent communication."
—David Cottrell

The vast majority of investment professionals make their money from the products they sell. Any good salesperson knows that to sell a product you have to find the right buttons to push so the customer will buy what you are selling. The next hot new manager. The next hot new stock. The next hot new technology. The next hot new . . . you can fill in the slot. People like to believe that they are getting the next hot new . . . whatever.

The problem with that way of investing is that there is very little talk about what you are trying to accomplish with your money.

The landscape changes when you work with someone in the other part of the business. Someone who has taken on a fiduciary role is required by law to act in the best interest of their clients, and the most important question to ask a client, if you are a fiduciary, is what they are trying to accomplish with their money.

Finding a client's risk tolerance is a big deal in our industry. A friend of mine once told me that we spend time trying to determine the maximum amount of risk that a client can stand and then forcing them to accept that risk for the rest of their lives. One of the great conundrums of our business is that we define risk based on how much an investment might move (standard deviation) over a one-year period of time, even though most investors are investing for very long periods with a lot of their money (think retirement and college). Risk over a long period of time looks much different than risk over a short period of time.

For instance, most people know that stocks carry the most amount of risk of the traditional investments, e.g., stocks and bonds. But it is important to remember that risk has two sides to it. There is upside risk and downside risk. I have never seen a client get mad because they realized upside risk.

No one has ever come to me and said, "You said that we were trying to earn 7 percent and we earned 10 percent this year and I am not happy about that!"

Investors get mad about realizing downside risk. When you look at downside risk, stocks have more than bonds over a short period of time but once you get out ten, fifteen, or twenty years, stocks have less downside risk than bonds. They still have more risk, it is just mostly upside risk.

If you are still with me, that would mean that stocks are safer than bonds over long periods of time. That is why time horizon is the first thing an investor should look at before investing. How long do you plan to invest your money? I suggest you think of your money in three buckets.

Bucket number one is money that you will probably need in the next eighteen months. Money with that short time horizon needs to be in cash or money market funds. Bonds and stocks can lose value in that short period of time, and if you need the money, you don't need to take market risk of any kind with your investments.

Bucket number two is money that you don't think you will need in the next eighteen months but may need in the next five to six years. That money needs to be in a diversified portfolio of bonds and stocks, but more heavily weighted in bonds than stocks. Bonds produce income and stocks fight inflation. Studies have said that the safest portfolio over that period of time would be around 30 percent in stocks and 70 percent in bonds.

Bucket number three is money that you don't plan to need for a while. On paper you would think that this bucket would be all stocks. There is certainly a case for that thought. But you have to remember, stocks may have very little downside risk over twenty years, but you have to survive twenty, one-year periods to get there, and stocks are all over the place year to year.

The key is to find a mix of stocks and bonds that can make the ride smooth enough for the investor to stick with the plan. Once you figure that out, you are ready to go.

RULE #45

Know When You Are Gambling

"Oh Lord, let me break even. I need the money."
—Gambler's Prayer

Most investors I talk with tell me how they want to have a better life, provide for a better life for their children, support their favorite charities, and not outlive their money. To be clear, they don't want to die early, they just want to have enough money to live longer.

Rarely do I talk to an investor older than forty that says, "I want to rock and roll! Let's go out there and put some money at risk!"

Nevertheless, a lot of investors find themselves in a cycle of risk-taking even though, in many cases, they are completely unaware. The large majority of the investment industry is made up of companies that sell investment products and the people that get paid to sell those products.

It's not inherently bad to get paid to sell products. Car dealers, clothing stores, electronic stores, and appliance stores often have salespeople that are paid a commission to sell their products. The problem in the investment world is that it is so hard for the investor to know who gets paid by the product and what they are getting paid.

Selling products at a high level requires certain skill sets, none of which has anything to do with connecting your goals and your investments. To sell products you need to:

- Be a good storyteller
- Understand the bells and whistles
- Be able to push the right emotional buttons of your client
- Be able to close the deal

If one product is better suited to your particular needs, but another product pays the advisor twice as much money to sell, has a cool story, and neat bells and whistles, too often the cool product with neat bells and whistles is the one that is recommended. It is understandable why that might happen. It is also easy to see how someone's portfolio of investments can get out of whack if that scenario plays out too many times.

The other challenge in working with someone who gets paid by the products they sell is that they have an incentive to move your money from one investment to another. If they get a commission to trade a stock, the only way to make more money off of that investment is to sell it. Then they can buy something else and get a commission off of that trade.

If someone has an annuity that has outlasted it penalty phase, a broker can sell it at no penalty and buy another annuity, receive a new commission, and start the penalty phase all over again. Good for the broker. Not so good for the client oftentimes.

Even our educational institutions encourage investors to gamble with their money. There are very few classes on investment philosophy, but there is the Stock Market Game which students can play through their school as early as middle school. You take play money and invest it for six weeks to see who can earn the most money. Six weeks is virtually never an appropriate holding period for an investment. They teach the lingo of trading securities, but rarely teach you the advantage of non-correlating assets or using index funds to lower your costs.

The financial press is no better. They report day to day activity in the markets as if it has some relevancy to your retirement plan investments, begging you to make a move in your portfolio.

The challenge is that the product selling side of the investment business is much more exciting than the fiduciary side, where products pay nothing to the adviser and no one is calling you up with really cool stories about really neat investments.

If you want to be pitched really cool stories and you want to manage the risk you take on your own, more power to you.

My concern is with those people who don't want that kind of relationship and don't want that kind of risk in their investment life, but are getting it anyway because it is so hard to tell the difference between those who sell products for a living and those who don't.

RULE #46

Understand Tracking Error And How To Use It

———

ule #5 is "Interest is a Weapon," which can be used for good or for bad. Tracking error has the same dynamic even though tracking error is not nearly as well known. Tracking error is a number that lets an investor know how closely his or her investment tracks a like index. For example, if you have a portfolio of large cap US stocks, you can look at how your portfolio tracks the S&P 500, an index of large cap US stocks.

Technically, tracking error is determined by subtracting the standard deviation of your portfolio by the standard deviation of the index you select for comparison. Standard deviation is the amount of movement up and down of a certain investment. It is not necessary to understand the formula behind tracking error, but it is important to understand what it means.

Most investors love tracking error when their investments perform better than the index. That is the Holy Grail, isn't it? You get to tell everyone that you beat the market. You beat your friends.

You are a financial genius. But they don't feel the same way when their investments have large tracking error and underperform the index. That is simply unacceptable. You can't go to a party and let your friends know that you underperformed the index. What is the opposite of the Holy Grail?

That kind of mentality plays out in the marketplace all the time. When a mutual fund beats its index, people pour money into it. And when a mutual fund is down to the index, money pours out of it. No matter what your goal is for your investments, neither of those actions are probably right.

If you are in a diversified portfolio of investments and you are trying to get market-like returns from your portfolio, then you don't want tracking error. You don't want it on either side, up or down. Because if you are getting a lot of tracking error, something is wrong with your portfolio. The opposite is true for those investors that are trying to get outsized returns. The only way to get outsized returns is to have a lot of tracking error. The more you look like the index, the less likely you are to beat that index. That is just logic 101, but just because it is logical to act a certain way doesn't mean people will act that way.

Mutual fund managers know that if they stray too far from the index, they will have a bad year and lose investors' money to another fund. But many of them have pitched their managers as people who know how to beat the markets. Rule #30 is, "Passive Beats Active Almost All The Time." That is as much because investors simply will not put up with underperformance in order to get outperformance over time.

Can you imagine putting all of your hard-earned money with a money manager who decided to buy four stocks in your portfolio? You would think he was crazy. As soon as one of them underperformed you would question his ability, his sanity, and his commitment to you. But the fact is that it doesn't take many stocks to reach the level of diminishing returns.

My experience with the law of diminishing returns in investments tells me that a dozen stocks in the S&P 500, any dozen, will represent 90 percent plus of the return of the index. Nevertheless, managers often buy 150 or 200 different positions. They do that, I believe, because investors can't handle the tracking error associated with only owning a few stocks. The fact of the matter is that if you want to be a good money manager, you actually have to have money to manage.

So, if you really want to beat the markets, find investments with a lot of tracking error and hope it is the good kind. If you don't want to pursue outperformance and are happy getting average returns over long periods of time, buy the whole index in an index fund and pay a lot less in fees in the process.

_____

_____

_____

_____

_____

_____

_____

_____

_____

_____

_____

_____

_____

_____

_____

_____

_____

_____

_____

_____

_____

_____

_____

_____

_____

_____

_____

_____

_____

_____

RULE #47

The Pendulum Always Swings

"We're waiting for the pendulum to swing back again,
which I am absolutely confident it will."

—Don Bluth

There is an old saying, "The only two things that are certain are death and taxes." I feel that you could add Rule #47 to that list. The pendulum always swings. That seems to be true about a lot of things, but it is certainly true about the markets and those drivers that influence the markets.

Over the last one hundred years or so we know that the equity markets have averaged around 10 percent per year. That is something that, it appears, we can pretty much count on. I hear people say, "This time it's different." But that has never been the case.

The free market system seems to reward the ownership of companies, especially when you own all of them, with a return of around 10 percent. That has been true through the agricultural

185

society of the early 1900s, followed by the industrial society, the technology society, and now the service society that seems to drive American economics.

Interestingly, there has probably never been one single year when the equity markets returned exactly 10 percent. The markets continually return more or less. That is why we call investing a "reversion to the mean" business. If you look at the past ten years of equity returns, and they have averaged 14 percent, you can feel pretty confident that they are about to underperform because over long periods of time they average 10 percent.

How do you get to an average of 10 percent if you are at 14 percent? You underperform. There are a lot of experts that want to explain why this happens, but I would say, "The pendulum always swings." That is true for fixed income markets as well, but their long-term average is closer to 5 percent.

The pendulum swings in other ways that affect investments as well. If you look back, over time you can see a trend that has caused havoc in the securities markets and that has to do with politics.

Conservatives have traditionally wanted the government to stay out of regulating businesses. The battle cry is, "Give the private sector the opportunity to make money and they will do good things with it." That seems to be true to an extent. But at some point, business becomes too deregulated, especially in the banking industry. It allows greed to take over and that becomes a problem. That is, in my opinion, the catalyst for the stock market crash of 1929, the stock market crash of 2008, and many crashes, bear markets, and downturns in the stock market since we started keeping good records.

So, what happens when the markets crash? We began to regulate our way out of the crisis. And we regulate and regulate and regulate. We regulate ourselves to a point where, if you lent money to the bank and asked for it back in a loan, they probably couldn't give it to you. Once businesses can't get loans to finance their business, we cry, "Too much regulation!" and the pendulum begins to swing the other way.

I know that there are a lot of people trying to make a living by explaining to you what the stock market is about to do and why it is about to do it. They are smart and spend a great deal of time coming up with their ideas. And they are often wrong.

As I write about Rule #47, I look back on the past ten years of equity returns through the end of 2022. The US stock market has averaged 12.13 percent and international equities have averaged 4.59 percent. If we are a reversion to the mean business, and if the pendulum is going to constantly swing from a center point of 10 percent, then what has to happen to get US equities to 10 percent? What has to happen to international equities to get to 10 percent?

The pendulum always swings. It might not swing as fast or as far as you may want it to swing, but if you can find the center point and you can find the pendulum, then you can come up with a pretty sound investment plan.

RULE #48

We Are The World

"Globalization is simply opening the free marketplace to encompass the entire world."
—**P.J. O'Rourke**

There is a thing called Home Bias. Home bias means that people prefer things they are familiar with over those things that aren't familiar. People pick their team to win against better teams. They pick their favorite items at the grocery store over new brands that might be better. They invest in stocks of companies they know and use over companies that might have a better balance sheet, market share, or book-to-price ratio.

Mark Twain said, "Write what you know." People feel safe with the familiar. They are willing to bet on the familiar. But that doesn't always produce the best results. I went to Vanderbilt and for years when Vandy was in the NCAA Basketball Tournament, I picked them to go way too far. Once I even picked them to win.

189

Although, to my credit, I filled out two brackets that year in case I was wrong about Vandy . . . and I was.

Rule #28 is "Sometimes it's just not your fault." That's because we often use the wrong side of our brain to make decisions. The part of the brain called the amygdala promotes emotional decisions like picking Vandy to go all the way. The part called the pre-frontal cortex is used to make reasonable, objective, cognitive decisions.

Home bias starts with the amygdala. In investing, it manifests itself in having too much stock in your own country. This is especially a big deal for the United States where so many companies sell stock.

At the end of 2022, the US stock market accounted for 59 percent of all of the stocks available to trade in the world. The rest of the world only accounted for 41 percent. We are the big dog in the equity world. Other countries are hard to understand. Many times, their accounting systems are different. Their rules of business are different. The currency is different. There are just a lot of reasons why you would feel uncomfortable investing abroad.

But just because it doesn't feel right doesn't mean it's not a good idea. We are the world. We have become a global marketplace. We buy goods made in China, Taiwan, South America, Europe, and anywhere else that will make them cheaper or better than the US. A few years ago, I remember reading that the biggest imported car in the US was a Ford and the biggest car made in America was a Toyota. Globalization is here and I think it is here to stay.

So why would you choose to leave 41 percent of your stock choices off the table just because they didn't originate in the US? It is understandable but not reasonable. Markets have cycles. International cycles are different from US cycles. But over time, they both have about the same projected return. That is what diversification is all about: getting a certain return over time but using different investments to get there so they are not all down at the same time. Of course, that means that they are not all up at the same time either. When you put them together you still get the same return over time, but without all the volatility.

US stocks can outperform international stocks for a long time, such as we have seen in 2010 through 2020. But the opposite can also be true as the first ten years of the 2000s showed us. Years ago, to prove this point to an investor who wanted to buy only US stocks, I pulled out a book of returns over the past one hundred years. I asked him to pick random dates and we would look at the twenty-year time period after that date to see if international stocks had added value to a portfolio. He picked his mother's birthday, my mother's birthday, and presidential terms. Every date he picked showed that a balance of stocks around the world performed better than having a home bias. So just remember when you start building your portfolio, "It's a big world out there."

RULE #49

Investing Is Like Religion

"Carry your faith wherever you go, mix it with love and let it show. But keep your mind open as you move along. And always remember, you might be wrong."

aul Thorn is a singer, songwriter, painter, philosopher, and former-boxer extraordinaire. He is from my hometown, which is lucky for me as I may have never been able to call him my friend if he had been from somewhere else. But as is the case in most small towns, you get to know everyone. Paul's dad is a preacher and he has grown up in the Christian faith. But as with other great philosophers, Paul is willing to think about the fact that his idea of faith and religion may be wrong, yet he sticks with it.

One day after his song, "You Might Be Wrong," came out on his album, "Pimps and Preachers," it occurred to me that religion and investing have a very common thread. With religion, you pick one, you commit to it, and then, when you die, you find out if you were right. With investing you do exactly the same thing except that you find out just before you die. If you are still living and have run out of money, you realize that you might have been wrong.

Moving between different religions is a tough way of life that provides very little smooth sailing as you chart your life course. Changing your investment plan often is a great way to increase your odds of failure.

So how do you choose the right route for you? Well, I think you can use the same process to an extent. Choosing a religion usually comes down to how you were raised, history, evidence, and comfort level. And it really helps if you have a good preacher that you can trust as you go through life. Choosing an investment plan shouldn't be much different.

Most people that come through my doors have been shaped by the experiences of their parents and grandparents. It takes a bit of work to find out where their comfort level is with investing, and even a bit more time to understand what money actually means to them. Is it a safety net, a competition, or a conduit to better things? All of that matters to achieve the right outcome. But once you figure that out, the best plans are based on historical data, empirical evidence, and an ability to stick with the plan.

It takes discipline to commit to an investment plan for the long haul. It takes a lot of effort to use your pre-frontal cortex to make reasonable decisions when your amygdala is begging you to change course. But there is comfort in the fact that we have had over a hundred years of evidence that the free market system we invest in will produce certain results, regardless of the obstacles that we confront year in and year out.

The last point I will make is that you can make all of these decisions on your own. You can come up with your own plan and implement it without any help. But just like having a good preacher to lean on helps when your faith tends to waiver, your chance of success in investing is considerably higher when you have the right adviser to help you get back on track. And if you are having a hard time figuring that out, just go back to Rule #3 and read it again.

RULE #50

The Best Return Is Not Always The Biggest

"When all things are considered holistically, the best expected return on investment varies from client to client."

—Hendrith Vanlon Smith Jr, CEO of Mayflower-Plymouth

There are a lot of unintended consequences on the road to financial health. They can wreak havoc on a well-laid plan. I am closing in on four decades in the investment business and there are a few things that happen regularly that can have significant, unintended consequences.

For instance, someone will come to me and say, "I have been thinking about giving you some money to invest. I just can't make up my mind between you and some other people, so this is what I want to do. I am going to give each of you a third of the money

197

and we can look at how you have done at the end of the year and then I will decide who gets it all."

Now, that may seem like a smart thing, pitting a few experts against each other to see who comes out on top. But the problem is that you have just said that the person who earns you the most money will get the rest of it. What I have just heard from you is that goals don't matter. Risk tolerance doesn't matter. Appropriate investments don't matter. The only thing that matters is return.

You have pretty much guaranteed that all three of us will ignore those factors that might mean the most to your long-term success. We will just roll the dice and hope we win. You have all but guaranteed a high risk/high return or loss portfolio.

In all of my years investing for people, I have found very few clients who actually want or need a high-risk portfolio. But this focus on portfolio return as a way to gauge your success will get you just that.

What I have found to be the most important factors in building a proper portfolio have to do with how you feel. What does money mean to you? Is it a safety net or a score card? Does it represent opportunity or a chance to give back? When your portfolio goes down, at what point do you begin to want to change your plan? These are the things that can guide an adviser to create an appropriate portfolio. Understanding how our clients feel is key to keeping them on the path they have chosen to create financial health.

One of the secrets of the investment business is that it is not that hard to come up with a portfolio that will get our clients where they need to be, as long as their time horizon is long enough. But creating a portfolio that a client will stick with when they get scared or greedy is where the value of a great investment plan lies.

If you go for too high of a return over time, but can't emotionally handle the large swings in the portfolio on a day to day basis, then you will make mistakes and never get that target return. If you are working with a broker who gets paid by moving from one investment to another, and you are not keeping up with your portfolio, you may find your long-term plan is not where it should be and that a lot of your return has been eaten up in fees.

If you try to invest like your friends or someone you work with who seems successful, you may find that their goals and yours are different. What is right for them may not be right for you.

The fact is that there is only one you. How you feel about money and how that fits into your financial goals is something you and/or your adviser have to understand for you to be successful. That is a very personal thing.

At the end of the day, it doesn't matter what the markets are doing or what your best friend is doing. It doesn't matter if someone you know made more or less than you made last year. It matters that you are on the right track and you are willing to stay there.

That is how you win the investment race.

ACKNOWLEDGMENTS

I'm sure I could do something significant in my life without the help of my wife, Annette, and my two daughters, Dakin and Lilla, but it wouldn't be as significant. Annette knows me better than I know myself and her advice is always valuable when I am smart enough to take it. Not only is she the love of my life, but my partner in everything I take on.

Dakin and Lilla expect me to be great and demand the effort from me that it takes to make the attempt. I fail every day, but their love, encouragement, humor, and wit never wane. That trio of girls are the flame that keeps my life force lit. And, as with most families, we are expanding from those born in to those brought in. Hogan and Cannon are my surrogate sons and I am so glad they are a part of our lives.

Paul Mitchell is a massively talented marketing professional. He is a branding genius who came up with cover ideas for both *Top 40* and *Top 50*. Thanks for taking time from your real work and slumming with me to make me look good.

Corinne Fikes has been the person who has kept me going through my writings and speeches and presentations for the last seven years. She knows how to make me look good and she has such a steady hand when we need one. She has always believed in me and the feeling is mutual. She has made our firm look like the firm we aspire to be. And thank you, Dakin, for taking the baton from Corinne when she had her third child. I am sure I would have been lost if you hadn't run the last leg of this project with me.

Anita Giglio has been my editor for every piece of writing that has left my hands into the public domain for over three decades. We are a team and I simply cannot put into words what it means to have someone of her talent, faith, and trust on my side for so long. I make a lot of mistakes but I must be doing something right because she is still hanging in there with me.

Tom Dean is my publishing consultant and the force behind the idea of expanding my second edition to fifty rules. I guess he read the first forty and felt like I wasn't done yet. He has led me through this publishing maze and helped me settle in with Morgan James. I am grateful for his vision and his ability to see my vision.

Sarah Rexford is my editor on this project, and God willing, my next one as well. She is talented, efficient, and easy to work with. Critical elements when working with an author like me. She brought me to the finish line when I was having a hard time getting there.

And finally, the Morgan James crew who took me on for my 2nd Edition and hopefully a few more down the road. David, Jim, and Emily: thanks for putting up with me and helping me get my message to those that need it most.

In the last line of the poem "Invictus" by William Ernest Henley, he inspires us by saying, "I am the master of my fate, I am the captain of my soul." If this book can get you just a bit closer to being the master of your fate, then I am good with that.

ABOUT THE AUTHOR

Scott Reed, BCF, AIFA, CIMA, CEFEX Analyst, is the CEO of Hardy Reed, LLC, one of the nation's leading fiduciary advisory firms. Scott has become one of the most respected and entertaining voices in the investment world regarding fiduciary excellence and investment ethics.

From speaking at national and regional conferences across the country, to helping rewrite the Code of Ethics for the Investment and Wealth Institute, he has become known as a voice of reason in an industry that has struggled with the conflict between doing what is right for its clients and what is profitable for the business.

Scott has served as Chairman of the Board of Directors for the Center for Board Certified Fiduciaries as well as Chairman of the PACE committee of the Investment and Wealth Institute, which oversees the Promotion and Advancement of Certification Excellence for the designations promoted by the Institute.

Scott has served on over thirty non-profit boards, giving him the unusual perspective of client and advisor. He has written a syndicated financial column focused on investment philosophy for over three decades. Scott graduated from Tupelo High School and Vanderbilt University. He lives in Tupelo, Mississippi, with his wife Annette. They have two daughters, a son-in-law, an almost son-in-law, and two dogs.

Outside of his duties as CEO, Scott is continuing to write with two non-fiction books and one fiction book on the drawing board.

TO VISIT SCOTT'S WEBSITE AND VIEW EDUCATIONAL VIDEOS, SCAN THE QR CODE BELOW!

A free ebook edition is available with the purchase of this book.

To claim your free ebook edition:

1. Visit MorganJamesBOGO.com
2. Sign your name CLEARLY in the space
3. Complete the form and submit a photo of the entire copyright page
4. You or your friend can download the ebook to your preferred device

A **FREE** ebook edition is available for you or a friend with the purchase of this print book.

CLEARLY SIGN YOUR NAME ABOVE

Instructions to claim your free ebook edition:
1. Visit MorganJamesBOGO.com
2. Sign your name CLEARLY in the space above
3. Complete the form and submit a photo of this entire page
4. You or your friend can download the ebook to your preferred device

Print & Digital Together Forever.

Snap a photo

Free ebook

Read anywhere